LIVING CREATION

Poetry

Perennia
Early Poems
Experimental Sonnets
Madrigals
Poetry of Francis Warner
Lucca Quartet
Morning Vespers
Spring Harvest
Epithalamium
Collected Poems 1960–1984

Plays

Maquettes (a trilogy of one-act plays)
Lying Figures (Part One of REQUIEM, a trilogy)
Killing Time (Part Two of REQUIEM)
Meeting Ends (Part Three of REQUIEM)
A Conception of Love
Light Shadows
Moving Reflections
Living Creation

Editor

Eleven Poems by Edmund Blunden
Garland
Studies in the Arts

LIVING
CREATION

a play by Francis Warner

Chloris eram quae Flora vocor

Ovid, *Fasti* V. 195

OXFORD THEATRE TEXTS 8

COLIN SMYTHE, GERRARDS CROSS, 1985

British Library Cataloguing in Publication Data

Warner, Francis
Living creation.—(Oxford theatre texts,
ISSN 0141–1152; 8)
I. Title   II. Series
822′.914   PR6073.A724
ISBN 0–86140–227–8

First published in 1985 by Colin Smythe Ltd.
Gerrards Cross, Buckinghamshire

Distributed in North America by Humanities Press Inc.
171 First Avenue, Atlantic Highlands, N.J. 07716

Photographs and cover design by Billett Potter of Oxford

Plates of Botticelli's paintings are published
by kind permission as follows :

'Primavera', 'Birth of Venus', and 'Pallas and the Centaur' :
Uffizi, Florence; (© Scala)
'Magdalene at the Foot of the Cross (Mystic Crucifixion)' :
Fogg Art Museum, Cambridge, Mass.
'Mars and Venus' and 'Mystic Nativity' :
National Gallery, London

Produced in Great Britain

All enquiries regarding performing rights should be addressed to the publishers.

LIVING CREATION was commissioned jointly by the Oxford High School for Girls and the Oxford University Experimental Theatre Club. Additional sponsorship was also given by the Oxford University Players (University College). It was first performed on Thursday, 21st March, 1985. The director was Greta Verdin.

The cast was as follows:

Women

Clotho	*Signe Biddle*
Lachesis	*Teresa Morgan*
Atropos	*Vivien Foster*
Salvestra	*Emily Fuller*
Albiera	*Lucy Warner*
Marietta	*Bridget Foreman*
Simonetta Vespucci	*Francesca Lepper*
Clarice Orsini de' Medici	*Ayesha Vardag*
Riguardata	*Alex Oldroyd*

Men

Lorenzo de' Medici	*Mark Payton*
Giuliano de' Medici	*John Clargo*
Sandro Botticelli	*Martin Whitworth*
Domenico Ghirlandaio	*Max Hill*
Giorgio Vespucci	*Simon Cowley*
Marsilio Ficino	*Tim Prentki*
Francesco de' Pazzi	*Tim Hudson*
Angelo Poliziano	*Adam Petalas Miranda*
Savonarola	*Robert Wynford Evans*
Doffo Spini	*Tim Hudson*
Herald	*Simon Walker*

Non-speaking parts:

Alex Broome, Francis Corrie, David Gautrey, Michael Heath, Edward Leach.

Stage Manager Caroline Mayr-Harting. Costumes and horses R.S.C., Sheila Wright, and Diana Clark. Banners Andrew Crisp. Dance arranged by Mary-Clare de A'Echevarría. Lighting Design David Colmer.

Characters

Clotho ⎫
Lachesis ⎬ The Three Fates
Atropos ⎭

Lorenzo de' Medici
Giuliano de' Medici
Clarice Orsini de' Medici
Angelo Poliziano
Marsilio Ficino
Giorgio Vespucci
Sandro Botticelli
Domenico Ghirlandaio
Francesco de' Pazzi
Savonarola
Doffo Spini
Herald
Simonetta Vespucci
Salvestra
Albiera
Marietta
Riguardata

The play is set in Florence during the fifteenth century. There are two acts.

Act One

PROLOGUES

CLOTHO

We, robed in white with garlands on our heads,
Are the three daughters of Necessity,
Our Mother. Married domesticity
Cannot be ours. I spin the present threads
Of each and every one of you alive.
Yes, it was I, Clotho, the youngest, whom
You cried to when you first sparked in the womb :
To the bee-hive of birth made you survive.
(Indicating Lachesis)
Look to your past ! Lachesis on her throne
Allotted all your chances; in her lap
Are sample lives for you to choose. The map
Of life is hers, the voyage is your own.
    The future lies with Atropos, who hears
    No plea. She cuts each life's thread with her shears.

LACHESIS

Look to your past! For in it you will find
Mankind's destruction has been faced before.
We need not always weep. To overawe
Is easy. To reply, shake off, unbind
Is the great challenge. Listen, now; and learn.
In thirteen forty-seven, in the Crimea,
A trading-post of Genoese, in fear,
Besieged by Kipchak soldiers, would not turn
Its loyalty. The Kipchaks took the town
By catapulting plague-blown corpses in.
Sick galleys fled to Sicily : and down
To Egypt, up through France, Austria, Spain,
England, the Baltics, Sweden, to the snow
That Black Death cut one third of Europe's skein.

ATROPOS

One in three humans putrefied, to burn,
For that one act of evil. Persevere!
This time we know the consequence. I shear
According to your acts. From that dark urn,
In spite of all, some beauty rose, refined
To rarest life-enhancing wonder, for
(Coming downstage, and laying aside her shears)
Our Chaucer's laughing, ever-open door
Of love, and lust, and ladies was defined
By that extermination, and the glow
Learned from a golden city's impish brain—
The plague-racked Florence of Boccaccio.
Tonight we leave behind this origin
Some hundred years. Florence's dome, red-brown,
Crowns young Lorenzo's city here. Begin!

SALVESTRA *and* ALBIERA *dressing each other.*

SALVESTRA   God hold me in His love, no. I'm too shy!
Luca, my husband—

ALBIERA   Look, Salvestra, we
Are both sixteen; but I'm not married yet!
Doomed from the start. I knew that this would
    happen!
I've tried to do the right thing. All my friends
Stood round while I was fetlocking my horse
And urged me on : 'Yes; you must send it!' So
I did. And look what I've lost!

SALVESTRA   Albiera—

ALBIERA   What a price to pay! I'd given him a short
Sharp spur; and now I've lost him!

SALVESTRA   He will learn.
You've paved the way for his next girlfriend.

ALBIERA   Ugh!
I'll take a twitch to all those primping mares!

SALVESTRA   The game's not over yet.

ALBIERA   You bet it's not!
My brain has tongue attached. But don't you see?
Because I haven't got him any more,
I want him? But I can't now ask him back.
He'd not respect me. And, well : if he came,
I would lose interest. And he's just the same.
That's why he wants me.

Enter to them MARIETTA.

MARIETTA   Aren't you ready yet?
Albiera, now you've come to Florence,
Forget damp Naples. Join the Medici dance,
Gaze at the jousters round young Giuliano,
And crop new friends among that waving gold.

SALVESTRA   Ah! Marietta. Don't encourage her
To burn her eyesight on magnificence.
They live too high—but we can join the crowds!

MARIETTA   And dance, Salvestra, till our laces pinch.
The evening star defeats the setting sun :
Nothing's impossible to seizing minds
With chance, right time and place . . .

SALVESTRA   And God's good gift!

MARIETTA   These rusty tears that drizzle down your cheeks,
Albiera, must be sparkled into gems;
For here in Florence on the Baptist's day
Trumpets, innumerable viols and flutes,
Banners and stamping horses, sweets, and wine,
Dresses that make the silkworm hide its head,
And pageantry to steal the world's acclaim,
All this is ours. We walk our silver streets
And each shop flaunts its wealthiest merchandise,
Jostling the next in gorgeous ostentation
To grip the eye and shake a sudden blink.
Our sleeves brush gold. Pearled shoes tread the far
    East.
Our heads are crowned with garlands from the
    fields,
While higher ladies bend in dazzling crowns,
Their husbands' riches heavy on their necks.
All crowd to Santa Croce's piazza
And spread in circles. There, the highest row,
Is for the mighty. Next, in front, for those
No longer apt for gracefulness. Below
Is, waiting, ours; strewn with midsummer flowers
For us to weave, young women who will please
The courtesy of music with our steps.
First . . . Look! Here prance the jousters!

Enter behind her, taking her by surprise, SANDRO.

SANDRO   Marietta!

MARIETTA   Sandro!

SANDRO   You and your soft companions missed the bright
Armour on horseback charging a Saracen
That, hit, swings round and clouts the rider down!
The horses first were dressed in white; then blue.
Each rider stood up in his saddle, cantered,
Thrusting a dart to tease the quintain round;
Then, having measured pace and height, returned
To lift from liveried friends his battering lance;
Charge at full gallop at the Saracen,
And wheel to break his golden weapon under
The window'd lady of his fancy's choice.
Not all stayed on!

SALVESTRA   Sandro and Albiera!
Lorenzo's younger brother, like a star
Shining in silver armour rich with jewels!

SANDRO   That horse he rides is from Urbino's duke.
No one but he may mount that flawless strength.

Enter FRANCESCO DE' PAZZI.

FRANCESCO   Too high too young. Not everyone who bends
Acknowledges subordination to
The proud Medici.

SANDRO   Ah, Francesco, you
Surely owe much to them! The great Cosimo,
Lorenzo's grandfather, bought for your house
Its honour back. Set up your family's bank;
Gave you the friendship of his Holiness
Sixtus, over Imola. Your high rôle,
Treasurer to the Holy See, was once
Lorenzo's.

FRANCESCO   But he did not please the Pope :
                 Held back some forty thousand ducats which
                 We noble Pazzi gave the See of Rome.

ALBIERA   Lorenzo's favourite sister, Bianca :
                 Isn't she married to your family?
                 Surely you're a Medici brother-in-law!

FRANCESCO   Enough! This boy of twenty-one grows fast.

SANDRO   God grant his youth and rising fortunes last!

SCENE TWO

Exit FRANCESCO. *Enter* GIORGIO VESPUCCI *and*
DOMENICO.

VESPUCCI   Sandro, we hoped to find you here today
                 Feeding the eagles as elusive honour
                 Is courted by the heavy sweat of steel.
                 Prince Giuliano, twenty-one and lithe,
                 Rides with a man-at-arms who lifts up high
                 The banner of Alexandrian taffeta
                 That you have painted. It shows swiftest thought
                 Transfigured by imagination—
                 A life-size lady in a suit of gold
                 Down to the knee, her feet on flowers of fire;
                 In her right hand a lance, and in her left
                 Medusa on a shield.
                 Medici olive binds god Cupid's hands
                 With glistening cord, while, over all, the sun
                 Shines above Pallas' hair entwined with flowers
                 Lifting the wind.

DOMENICO   My dear and fellow painter.
                 It is not lost on us that Pallas' face
                 Is Simonetta—Giuliano's dream;
                 Marco Vespucci's wife since sweet sixteen.

VESPUCCI   Your banner for young Giuliano's joust
             Does us great honour, Sandro. We Vespucci,
             And this girl-Venus wafted to our shore,
             Our cousin Marco's wife, thank you. May we
             Commission a fresco of great Saint Augustine
             On the right of our door through to the choir
             At All Saints' Church?

SANDRO   What's on the left-hand side?

VESPUCCI   Domenico Ghirlandaio here has sworn
             To paint Saint Jerome as a cardinal.

SANDRO   Do you intend we two shall paint together?

DOMENICO   You daub on your side and I'll glow on mine.

SANDRO   Domenico paints the books, and I the faces?

DOMENICO   What! Play the shadow to your excellence?
             I'll be beheaded first.

VESPUCCI   Well? May we talk?
             Come to my garden when tomorrow wakes
             And pluck agreement from my gratitude.

             Exit VESPUCCI.

SANDRO   Domenico, my mocking friend : you rogue!

DOMENICO   Have the Medici paid you?

SANDRO   No, not yet.

DOMENICO   Bills can be cleared!

SANDRO   The money's richly needed!

DOMENICO   You live at chance; your spirit of recklessness
             Swerves in your flowing lines.

SCENE THREE

MARIETTA, SALVESTRA, and ALBIERA *return.*

MARIETTA   The approaching trumpets!

SALVESTRA   Sandro, you love all women. Why are you still
A thirty-year-old bachelor?

DOMENICO   He stinks.

ALBIERA   No more than freshness on an April day.

SALVESTRA   (*Playfully*) We love you.

SANDRO   Ladies, the Medici come!
At thirteen I was taught my trade by Fra
Filippo Lippi. From him I learned to love
All physical beauty, grave and exquisite.
His skittled models were less grave. The nun
Spinetta, who bore him our Filippino,
So woke my teen eyes that if now I dream
I'm married, I leap out of bed and wash;
Scour out my brain, rather than sleep again.
Night-walking Florence.

ALBIERA   You must taste the bit
To harness beauty. Stable oats in straw
Can never nourish like good provender.

SALVESTRA   Albiera! They say your workshop home
Is full of idle, joking wits; young men
Who should be working; studying; in the church!

ALBIERA   Only the thin, blind spectre loneliness
Will stoop your bed and brush each cheek with grey
When death, with skilful fingers, finds your veins
And skeins the pulling silk of life away.

Trumpets. A HERALD.

HERALD   On this day, the twenty-eighth of June, in the year
           of Our Lord 1475, during the midsummer octave
           and in celebration of the Nativity of Saint John the
           Baptist, patron saint of this beautiful city of
           Florence; and also to celebrate and commemorate
           the alliance, successfully concluded this winter past,
           between the noble cities and citizens of Venice
           (*Trumpet*), Milan (*Trumpet*), and Florence
           (*Trumpet*), Lorenzo de' Medici sponsors this
           festival; to the greater glory of God, and to the
           success of this pact of peace.

           Trumpets. Applause.

SALVESTRA There's Simonetta taking up her place
           Dressed as the Queen of Spring. Hear the applause!
           She's trembling; leans down on her lady's arm.
           Marco's away, abroad. Giorgio Vespucci
           Guides her to take the centre of the stands.

MARIETTA   She's never looked more beautiful. Through tears
           All men must love her.

SALVESTRA   The piazza's seething
           With bodies as they part to let pride through.
           Count Robert's sons, the Sanseverino brothers—
           Gianfrancesco and dark Gaspare.
           Now a magnificent Venetian knight
           Holds a white ensign—gold lion of Saint Mark.
           Next prance eight brothers of the Nerli, crowding
           Their champion Benedetto. A grim flag,
           Frowning Apollo strangling the serpent, flaps.
           Luigi della Stufa, his father, and brother . . .

MARIETTA   And Piero di Jacopo Guicciardini on
           A night-black charger

SANDRO   Called Cavalieri . . .

ALBIERA   Who now? Why, there! Is that Lorenzo's brother?

MARIETTA The last, our Giuliano; prince of youth.
Impossible to say how many gems
Shimmer his pearled companions. Diamonds
Steal from the light and blind it back for sport
All down his cloak.

SALVESTRA   He's thrown it to the crowd!
They fight for jewels! And now his armour is
Of beaten silver entire.

SANDRO   Verrocchio's helmet!

MARIETTA Is it Minerva?

SANDRO   Plumed.

ALBIERA   Ah! See his lance!

SANDRO   He bows to Simonetta. She throws down
Her favour. A boy page has picked it up;
Tosses it to him. He catches it, and bows
Once more to her, and wears it round his arm.

ALBIERA   Who walks behind, soberly dressed, alone?

SANDRO   Magnificent Lorenzo, with no need
Of jewels today. He holds all in his eyes.

MARIETTA In compliment to his young brother, he
Follows on foot, austere; his father's son,
Cosimo's grandchild . . .
Though only twenty-five, he rules us all.
The greatest of our age.

SALVESTRA   No foreigner
Of any name or note passes through Florence
Without first seeking out his courtesy
And deft protection.

ALBIERA   Is he married?

MARIETTA   To
           The red-haired Roman, Clarice Orsini.
           Her uncle is the Cardinal Latino.

SALVESTRA Some say sweet Giuliano will become
           One to receive the envied wide-brimmed hat.

ALBIERA   Oh what a waste!

                    SCENE FIVE

           Enter CLARICE ORSINI *and* LORENZO.

           Trumpet.

CLARICE   Lorenzo, dearest, pause
           With me, your wife, before you once more show
           Authority to have a fragrant face.

LORENZO   My summer sky, habitual company,
           Mother of our three infants, and my joy;
           Do you remember our wedding-joust, when you
           Came, the pure, young Orsini bride from Rome,
           While we were both nineteen, six years ago?
           Dressed in brocade of white and gold, riding
           The black war-horse given by proud Naples' king
           Ferrante? And your dazzling Florence mantle?
           The fifers and the trumpeters in front,
           My Carlo and Tommaso close behind
           To guard you and protect, while all around
           Your waving field of bridesmen walked beside?

CLARICE   Your brother Giuliano brought me here
           To you from Monterondo; he has earned
           This great day's honour. But, dear husband, I
           Also remember when, four months before
           Our wedding-day, while I was still in Rome,
           You gave a joust in this same piazza

To celebrate our coming joy, at which
You wore the favour of another girl;
And wrote her poems—Lucrezia Donati.

LORENZO   Clarice; she was all eleven years old.

CLARICE   Lucky for you; and her. And did you win?

LORENZO   Though I had no great skill, and was still young,
The first prize was awarded me, a helmet
Silver-inlaid, crested with the god Mars.

CLARICE   Ah, my Lorenzo; leave the city soon
Before you are unable to relax
From cares of state. Play with our five-year-old.
She misses you—and I am three months pregnant.
I never minded you called her Lucrezia.
Here is three years of energy incarnate,
Piero. Take him fishing. Lift Maddelena
High on your shoulders as she loves. Come, ride
Through our pine-scented Mugello. The gardeners
Wait your decisions on their planting, while
Your farmers need to see you. At Careggi
Calabrian pigs of yours breed. Poggio holds
Golden pheasants you beckoned from Sicily.
The rare hares have arrived with twitching mouths
From Tunis, with gazelles: and now (God help me!)
Some apes and parrots have been shipped in from
The Sultan of Babylon, with a giraffe!

LORENZO   It is so gentle it will take an apple
From Maddelena's shrimp-pink hand. You're right;
I'll come. The hunting-dogs from Mantua—
Are they well exercised?

CLARICE   Yes, by Matteo
Franco, our poet.

LORENZO   One of the first, and dearest—
After the family—of all our household.
He's a good poet, a fair rival to
Luigi Pulci.

CLARICE   Matteo insists I rest.

LORENZO   Good! You must have no more miscarriages.
                 This one may become Pope.

CLARICE   With you all things
                 Are possible. The plague rages in Pisa.
                 Come to us soon where your green mountain-side
                 Blends with an air so pure, mild evening's light
                 Lingers beyond its time, hears Vespers' bell,
                 Looks back like Orpheus, as loath to leave
                 And lose the day; then suddenly is starred.

LORENZO   The city claims me.

CLARICE   Yes; I'll leave you now.
                 Good luck; Here comes your wisest friend and
                     guide.

                 Exit CLARICE.

                         SCENE SIX

                 Enter FICINO.

LORENZO   Marsilio Ficino, teacher, friend,
                 How are your bones today?

FICINO   Don't ask me that,
                 Lorenzo. Not one day in my whole life
                 Has been quite free from pain.

LORENZO   That's not like you!
                 Gloomy? Where is your wit? Come—joust and
                     dance!

FICINO   I'm just a gloomy old Dominican friar
                 Living in splendour of Europe's greatest clan.

LORENZO   Yes, reconciling Plato with sweet Christ,
                 We know. Now, what of Giuliano's armour?

FICINO   This open air, heavy with scent and pollen,
             The soft glow of the sun; the lutes and viols!

LORENZO   The coursers are pawing the ground at the
                  starting-place!

FICINO   Your celebrations bring the flower of youth
             To earthly beauty. Man's end, here on earth,
             Is to make pleasure one with wisdom.

LORENZO   We do!
             Look! The Greek gods enhance the Baptist's Day!
             This horsemanship sharpens all concentration;
             Strengthens weak muscles; thrills and delights the
                  crowd.
             My family grows more admired, and loved;

             SANDRO *passes.*

             And painters, poets, all, all benefit.
             Sandro! Come here. Ficino tells us pleasure
             And wisdom can be one.

SANDRO   And so they can;
             But how? That is my problem.

FICINO   With three angels:
             Beauty, Truth, Proportion. Flee excess!
             Be happy in the present.

LORENZO   And so we are!

             Exit SANDRO.

FICINO   Lorenzo, listen. The Pope is ripe with anger
             Because you have forbidden his Francesco
             Salviati to take possession of
             The archbishopric of Pisa.

LORENZO   That offence,
             If it is one, has been committed by

The whole of Florence, No, the Signoria
Does not want Salviati. Sixtus claims
Letters supporting him have come. If so,
They come from disaffected outcasts, and
For just that reason would divide and wreck,
And must be spurned.

FICINO   Lorenzo, hasten slowly.
Your retrospective law, setting aside
Female claims of those whose fathers die
Intestate, has provided your close friends,
Old Borromeo's nephews, with vast wealth
At the expense of Beatrice de' Pazzi,
His thoughtful daughter. The Pazzi cannot love
you.

LORENZO   Bianca, my own perfect sister, is
The wife of Guglielmo. He's our man.

FICINO   One Pazzi does not speak for all. Clear Time
Is, by its nature, fluid, slippery,
And ever-changing. Held, it evaporates.
Ridden and groomed, then freed, it works for you,
And every generation brings afresh
New innocence. Be generous to all—
Remember your father's magnanimity—
Not just to friends. Water boxed in grows stale.

LORENZO   My thought's musician; help me find the grail.

LORENZO *takes up his formal position as Lord of the
Joust.*

SCENE SEVEN

LORENZO   Even as the opening fig upon the branch
Gives out three tongues of fire, yet all are one,
So Milan, Venice, Florence, now become
United, but look out upon the world
Three ways. On this historic Baptist's Day,
Feast of our patron saint who guards us from

The plague, blesses us with prosperity,
As sunshine dances on their armour jewels
We welcome our proud guests and pay them
      homage.
Each one of us lives in the eye of Heaven.
My grandfather Cosimo, and my father,
Bequeathed us peace. All now are carefree, young
And clear in spirit, for the future holds
Promise sure as sunrise, and you shall breathe
A fresher air under a wider sky.
Milan has honoured us. Now, to complete
Our tournament, Venice and Florence joust.
Welcome, Serenissima's knight-at-arms,
In your Venetian, golden coat of mail!
For our part, no one less than my loved brother
Shall carry high our city's fleur-de-lis.
Herald, prepare! Let the last joust begin!

Trumpet.

HERALD
The Baptistery holds our offerings.
All must stand back! Let the two combatants
Have room each to prepare to meet the other.
Our Standard-bearer of Justice and eight Priors
Decree, as only the Signoria can,
No one shall touch the lists on pain of death.
Condottiero, with the sacred bones
Of Saint Mark in your flag, lion of Venice,
Secure your helmet, take up your jousting-lance,
And show your skill upon the Baptist's Day.

SIMONETTA
Forgive my tears. Last night I lay awake
Longing for Time to jump and find my Julio
Safe in my arms. Why did he choose to fight
With so experienced a juggernaut?
What if he falls? Oh, please God let this pass!
But if he wins, what on earth do I say?
I dread to make a speech to all this crowd.

VESPUCCI
You stand costumed as Queen of Spring, and—
      yes—

You are her incarnation! Simply say
What's in your heart. But if he falls, be silent.

FRANCESCO   Giorgio Vespucci standing by her side
Is a close friend of the Medici gang,
One of Ficino's mad Academy.
What kind of a Republic is this, now
Those tyrants dominate the lives of all?
Young Simonetta may think that she's Spring,
Marco her husband being far away,
But Marco's brother, Piero, feels defiled
And bears a grudge. May Giuliano fall!

ALBIERA   You're a pugnacious little bachelor.

MARIETTA   Keep well away from him. He has crow's feet
Under his eyes. Were the Medici gone,
He thinks his Pazzi clan would fill their place.

DOMENICO   Sandro; do you think one day I'll be known
As the first artist, the first of our age,
To paint a figure wearing spectacles?

SANDRO   Yes; that's about your limit. Giuliano
Bows to the Herald—look! His plumes are raised.

HERALD   The flag of Florence, dear and noble city,
Today is carried in Medici hands.
Giuliano di Piero di Cosimo,
Secure your helmet; raise your jousting-lance,
And prove your knighthood on this Baptist's Day.

               Trumpet. They charge.

SANDRO   Julio's lance splinters to pine-needles
On the Venetian's shield!

DOMENICO   Julio's horse,
Orso, sinks at the impact. But, recovers!
That Venice battering-ram has snapped against
Our Giuliano's armour . . .

MARIETTA
         Kill! Tear down
The mouldy bones of thieved Saint Mark; that lion
Bright as the sun with his white ensign!

ALBIERA
            Stop them!
The horses foam and paw the stamping ground.
What are they doing? No! They're not stabbing!

FRANCESCO
                 No;
The golden knight has locked his arms around
The young Medici so he cannot move.

VESPUCCI
They're wrestling, arm to arm. Lorenzo stands!
Julio cracks the helmet of his foe
Like a stooped falcon plunging on his prey!

Trumpet.

SIMONETTA
Oh, God; oh, God! He's safe. They've parted now.
I'm trembling and can't stand.

HERALD
The Master of the Joust proclaims this verdict;
Each has fought well. High honour's earned by all;
And Giuliano wins the victory.

Tumultuous applause.

LORENZO
Flawless, the horsemanship of our great guests.
Venice, Milan, and Florence now are one.
Let all rejoice in our festivity,
With dancing, singing, banquets, graceful games
Where human forms, through which bright silks
   and gems
Convert themselves to spirit, may love peace
Sent down from Heaven throughout all Italy.
Redeunt Saturnia regna. Florence herself
Is Queen, and glories in our corporate joy,
Splendour, and confidence. Brother, accept
The laurel wreath from a Laurentian hand.

GIULIANO   Though little worthy of this great event
                  And honour; hot and out of breath; profoundly
                  Grateful to my horse, I gladly kneel.

                  GIULIANO *accepts the wreath.*

                  And here I vow, I'll keep no gorgeous prize,
                  Except this helmet. What new wealth is won,
                  I give it to the Foundlings' Hospital.
                  Brother, there are no words that I can say
                  To tell my thanks. To me you always have
                  Been the Augustus of our time and state.
                  This laurel wreath I here accept, to crown
                  The Lady of the Feast, our Simonetta
                  Whose loveliness reflects the Supreme Good
                  Beyond our transitory world, where life is born.

                           SCENE EIGHT

                  Crowning of SIMONETTA.

SALVESTRA   It makes the high saints weep to see such beauty!
                  Why! Only last week, in Volterra, a boy
                  Was born with a bull's head, three teeth, a horn
                  Like a rhinoceros. The top of his head
                  Was open like a pomegranate, bursting
                  With fiery rays. Its arms and legs were hairy;
                  And, bless my soul! its feet were simply claws!
                  It lived three hours. The midwife died of fright.

ALBIERA   A monster! Please . . . ! Will Simonetta speak?

MARIETTA   I know she's frightened : but—they're playing her
                      flutes.
                  The crowd begins to clap. No. Will she stand?
                  She hesitates, and blushes.

ALBIERA   *Please* say something!

                  SIMONETTA *rises.*

SIMONETTA   Sunrise now bathes the sleeping cheeks of all
Creation, making fresh the blush of spring,
Throwing a necklace of ten thousand stars
Over new green to hide her nakedness
With sudden showers and colours in the grass :
Daisies that wink at night and drop the head,
The sea-shore myrtle, mountain violet,
Snowdrops who fight the hard, teeth-chattering
    frost,
Crocus, and brave and dangerous aconite,
While mottled skies blow clearer with mild days,
Summon the blustering February winds
From March, to calm them with a poet's power
To make old young, re-shed the tears of things
Long past, call up the dead and beautiful
For our delight, and turn the seasons round.
April is here with all her gift of life
And spring runs riot now that winter dies.
Delicate, strong, with graceful dignity
She opens up, under the fires of heaven,
Freshness and wonder in each pulse that hides,
Swims, creeps or flies, bounds or parades or prowls :
The vulnerable wren twines her slight twigs;
From far, gust-skipping swallows have returned
Wing-fed on bias, to speak low to eggs;
Chaffinch, and all the company of air,
Mate, nest, and sing, while the white dress of light
Fills with the laughter of a grateful world,
With bold vitality of courting men
As women's merriment hops to and fro.
Now, as the queen of flowers, the rose, unfolds
The scented innocence of youth, disclosed
In early loveliness revealed, unspoiled,
That art, most beautiful of all our games
On earth, begins : the timeless dance of love.

The formal dance begins.

SCENE NINE

FICINO

The moving air, alive with trembling numbers,
Bows reverently, parting for its guests
The dancers, who embody harmony
And lift the stillness of a summer's day
Into sweet mathematics up to God.
When I am in my hillside home, the house
Cosimo gave me, and I look across
At your great villa of Careggio,
I often pray that the soul's harmony
For which I've searched so long may be revealed
To some rare painter, perhaps in our time;
Some supreme master of the single line
Who knows a sudden gesture, and each glance,
Are outward music of an inner song,
And can, holding our eyes and hands with wonder,
Leap into vision through imagined thought.

LORENZO

A poet of the brush—a painter's Dante?
Sandro, what do you say?

SANDRO

                                    If beauty is
A spiritual gift, it has most carnal
Consequences! For five years I have been
Guardian to the nun's son, Filippino.
Well! He may be your visionary soul,
Marsilio; one day he'll outshine me.
We hate in others faults we have ourselves,
And I have cured him of them. Great Lorenzo;
I have a gift to celebrate the triumph
Of this love-glowing tournament. May I
Present your brother with a golden dream
Shaped as the head-board for his naked bed?

LORENZO

Julio! Come and see your looking-glass!
(*To* SANDRO) Hold it up high; and let us guess its
        thought.

SANDRO *shows his picture 'Mars and Venus'.*

GIULIANO	Do I look that exhausted? Blow a shell To wake me up! Who's playing with my lance?
LORENZO	What are those bees that trepidate his hair?
FICINO	Sweetness and sting united, *discordia concors*: Venus tames Mars, but loves her opposite, And from their union Harmony is born. Poliziano, come!

Enter POLIZIANO.

LORENZO	Welcome! What's this?
POLIZIANO	Mighty Lorenzo; why, it's pure Lucretius! 'Oh Venus, Love : lull all the works of war On lands and seas to sleep, for only you Bring peace. Mars lies back, conquered by your wound.'
SANDRO	But do you like it? Here is Simonetta; This is his lance. Round Giuliano's head Are wasps from the Vespucci coat of arms. A pun upon their name : *Vespa*—wasp!
DOMENICO	(*Laughing*) Giuliano as Mars! His body is Pure Pollaiuoli, your old tutor; copied. The hands, and folds of the white dress, are good.
SANDRO	Copied? It certainly is not, you glib Hair-decorator's frog-spawn! May your gesso Crack in light frost! May all your colours change, Streak down your tempera, block up your nose, And make you thoroughly distempered!
LORENZO	Sandro, Forgive our rudeness. Thank you for this gift. I here commission you to dream in paint Ficino's reverie.

GIULIANO   We both are proud
That you are ours. Thank you for my bed's hope.

SANDRO   Magnificent Lorenzo, you I trust;
And Guiliano, you I honour—but
I'll use this board to crack this cackler's head!

                SANDRO *chases* DOMENICO *out with head-board of*
                'Mars and Venus'. The dance-music.

LORENZO   (*To* POLIZIANO) You go and calm him down.

                Exit POLIZIANO.

SCENE TEN

                                          Marsilio,
Tell me about that young man.

FICINO   Angelo
Poliziano, the astounding boy,
When sixteen sent to you the second book
Of Homer's *Iliad,* after your joust,
Translated elegantly from the Greek
Into hexameters of silver Latin
Smooth as a mole's coat.

LORENZO   Well, Clarice says
I need a tutor for my growing sprigs;
And a librarian. What is his background?

FICINO   He is a perfect poet, though his past
Is tragic. Twenty-one; an eldest child.
When he was ten his father had a cousin,
Cino, whose head was cracked by the del Mazza
Family, we call the Grancosi—
Crabby and cruel, vicious, belligerent.
Angelo's father called for punishment
On those who had maimed Cino, but himself
Was intercepted by them, walking outside

The walls of Montepulciano with
Two nephews, and his friend the shoemaker.
He fled. They caught him. He dropped down. His
  throat
Was sawn across.

LORENZO   Angelo shall be ours.
One eye seems large; the other small. His neck
Is twisted.

FICINO   And I have a hunched back. Yet
Beauty is longed for most by those who lack her.
Philosophy, by Argyropylos,
He has been taught; and your own poet-teacher,
Landino, made him skilled in rhetoric.

POLIZIANO *returns carrying the 'Mars and Venus'.*

POLIZIANO   Sandro is dancing with Landucci's wife,
Salvestra, alert as a sparrow at a trough
In snow.

LORENZO   Will you allow our patronage?
Be tutor to my children? Help my wife?
Care for and catalogue my precious books?

POLIZIANO   To build my nest inside your happy wood
Of laurel is my longed-for Golden Fleece.
Prince Giuliano, I will celebrate,
In stanzas, as our Sandro has in paint,
That beauty seated on the grass, your love,
The rose-cheeked Simonetta . . . Look! She leaves!
And this your Eden age, your joust, your skill,
As Luigi Pulci did for you, Lorenzo.

GIULIANO   Bring her to me, that she may see how Sandro
Has brought the wheat-gold music down her head
In waves across her shoulders to her breasts.

POLIZIANO   (*About to leave*) Your child Piero I will teach with
    care.

LORENZO   Ah! Since it is impossible to do
               Anything in this world all men will praise,
               Let us content ourselves to bring to birth
               Such things as satisfy a noble few
               Whose life and judgement we acknowledge good,
               And themselves win our admiration :
               This is true gentleness. No fault seems quite
               So bad when inexperience trims young years.
               Teach him to reach up high to worthy aims,
               To have compassion on the small, the frail,
               And to love life, living creation through
               His soul, his mind, his body, and each dusk
               Rip away darkness from the twinkling sky
               With faith in a new dawn, with enterprise
               The child of mastery's delighted strength.
               Go, with my blessing.

                      SCENE ELEVEN

               *Salvestra, Albiera, and Marietta sit at one outdoor
               table, Riguardata at another.*

SALVESTRA   The gorgeous Giuliano sent our poet
               To summon April, Simonetta, back.
               Let's kick our shoes, and drink this table's wine.

ALBIERA   In Naples, I love being at the farm
               All day, clumping around in flat-foot boots,
               Muddy, squelched, and wet; then, in the evening,
               Changing them for high, dainty, party shoes.

MARIETTA   Florence is dangerous to foreigners
               Who may not know our customs. See her feet?

ALBIERA   Why does she wear a bell high on her head?

SALVESTRA   Ah, Marietta, leave her innocence
               Unspoiled!

ALBIERA   Oh, no! No! Tell me, tell me all!

MARIETTA	Monna Riguardata; come and join us! Tell Albiera why you wear a bell.
RIGUARDATA	Oh! Are you new to Florence?
ALBIERA	Yes.
SALVESTRA	She's ours.
RIGUARDATA	You need not worry; I won't witchcraft her.
ALBIERA	We noticed your high shoes.
RIGUARDATA	Yes. Do you like them?
ALBIERA	I do.
RIGUARDATA	Then I will tell you how they feel.
MARIETTA	If glib Francesco joins us, I'll leave to Find what delay holds Simonetta back From all this waiting crowd. Ugh! Angelo Poliziano says that is a man Bog-steeped in vice, a practised promise-breaker Of every law both human and divine.

MARIETTA *leaves as* FRANCESCO *joins the group.*

FRANCESCO	The Medici always come out on top. Ah! Monna Riguardata. Please believe me, I have great sympathy for your flushed youth And shivering ideals. My dear Salvestra, Isn't she beautiful?
SALVESTRA	Worth ten of you.
FRANCESCO	I visit your apothecary's shop Your husband set up with your dowry at The Canto de' Tornaquinci—pay good money!
SALVESTRA	Leave her alone.

FRANCESCO   But she is public! Look!
Condemned to wear the high heels, gloves, and bell
By our appellate judge and Florence court.

ALBIERA   Oh! Is that what they mean!

FRANCESCO   Riguardata,
Though you are beautiful, and softly young,
You have not married well. Meo is crippled
In both an arm, and leg. Why! He's no man,
You know that better than us all. Just look!
Tawdrily dressed. You're badly shod. Your home
Has neither meat nor oil. A little bread,
And some light wine is all. No! I have never
Seen such a pretty girl share poverty
With so uncouth a husband. Riguardata:
I do have some compassion. I've decided
From now on you will be well clothed, and lack
Nothing your youth and beauty can require.
This hair will be as soft as Simonetta's.
Here; take my purse.

RIGUARDATA   I want . . . I want to stay
With my husband.

FRANCESCO   Don't make that final. Think!
You're poor. Your looks will soon be gone, ground
          down
In grief and drudgery. Don't waste your bloom.
Grow rich. Fine dresses, shoes, and a silk jacket
With belt; yes, every luxury abroad
Is yours, with leisure, if you'll work for me.

FRANCESCO *walks away some paces and becomes
absorbed elsewhere, waiting.*

SALVESTRA   What a suave viper, a despicable man!

RIGUARDATA   I feel like a caught fish thrown back, its throat
Torn by the hook.

ALBIERA   Because you were condemned
Once by the judge to wear these clothes of shame
For some despairing moment short of cash,
You need not go with him. Think what will
    happen!

SALVESTRA   Next time they'll whip you through the streets of
    Florence,
Or shut you in the Convent of Penitents!

RIGUARDATA   The Pazzi have the power to seize, and torture—
Expel—my Meo! (*Pause*) And I liked her hair.
(*Slowly rising*)
Mankind's a garden where all fresh plants grow,
And even weeds need rain.

> RIGUARDATA *leaves the table, and slowly goes over
> to* FRANCESCO, *to take his arm. They leave.*

ALBIERA   I can't believe it!

SALVESTRA   Bland insinuate!
With stroking and deceitful words, he parted
Her weak irresolution with his will.

ALBIERA   If you can make another say : 'What if . . . ?'
He or she's undermined half-way to hell.

SALVESTRA   Francesco and his business friend Bandini
Know nothing of the strength and courtesy
Of customary values, soon-lost paths
To our uncertain, longing search for God's
Will in our life.

> MARIETTA *returns.*

MARIETTA   I passed him. He's already sold her to
The public brothel. Simonetta's ill.

Lorenzo's sent Stephano, his own doctor.
Her breathing's dusty.

ALBIERA   Oh no! We must help her!
           Where is she?

SCENE TWELVE

DOMENICO *and* SANDRO.

DOMENICO   Sandro! What did Vespucci say?

SANDRO   He'll pay half now, if I will guarantee
          A fresco Saint Augustine on the screen
          At All Saints' Church; with cloak, armillary sphere
          Of the wide heavens; the grave saint's thoughtful
               head
          Showing absorption's subtlety of mind—
          And, on the architrave, of course, a shield
          Bearing the wasps of the Vespucci clan.

DOMENICO Right! For my Jerome as a Cardinal
          On the left side, I'll have an hour-glass,
          Ink-horn and pen, jars, books, glass water-bottles,
          Scissors, pounce-box, candlestick; *spectacles*!

SANDRO   We'll pace each other. Ah! This time I'll study
          The dead Andrea Castagno's craftsmanship;
          Pallaiuoli's tutor. Mine you mock.
          This earns me time to try Ficino's challenge
          To paint the dance of our soul's harmony
          Glimpsed through the seasons of this passing world.

SCENE THIRTEEN

Enter to the crowd ANGELO POLIZIANO, *on high.*

POLIZIANO   Darken the city : Simonetta's dead.
Carry her on a dark bier, as tears flood,
Whose whiteness was suffused with her sweet blood
Like lilies mingled with the rose's red.

Death today claims from lost hope's last caress
Her gentle laughter, truth, and dignity,
Her shyness, unaware simplicity,
And all her first youth in its loveliness.

Yet what she gave so far outshone the noon
Of high ambition, so outstripped the race
Of worldly thoughts, it caught the ancient tune
That struck the Sirens dumb, but left no trace.

Enter SIMONETTA, *carried on an open bier through
the audience, slowly, up to the centre, followed by*
GIORGIO VESPUCCI *and* FICINO. *Bell tolling.*

FICINO   She passes from our shadows into light.
Dear Giorgio; withdraw into your soul.
She who, so beautiful, was dear to you
You will find there, through the Divine Creator,
Far, far more lovely in her Maker's form
Than ever in her own. Yield all to God.
He alone is eternal life, and lifts
Sorrows, in death, from his loved worshippers.

VESPUCCI   Thank you for consolation. Here, today,
Upon her corpse I vow myself to God.
From this hour on I yield my classic mind
Up, to be priest, to Christ.

FRANCESCO   *(To Domenico)* Hear Angelo?
What's this about her truth? Her truth to whom?
Whose was she? Giuliano's, or her husband's?

DOMENICO   What was it? Poison?

FRANCESCO   No; just nervous asthma.
                  She choked breath on her pillow.

                  Enter on high to receive the procession of the bier,
                  LORENZO *and* GIULIANO.

GIULIANO   All my dear friends:
                  I have no words. Grief closes round my eyes
                  And weighs my tongue, now Simonetta's dead.
                  She, like a Venus, rose up through the waves
                  Of Florentines, blown here from Genoa.
                  Each barefoot step she pressed upon the grass
                  Imprinted flowers that grew where she had passed,
                  And left in every heart a sense of spring.
                  (*Bending to kiss the corpse*)
                  Chrysalis of eternity, goodbye.
                  (*Closing her eyes*)
                  Your brief hour lived, for ever close each eye.
                  Winter has come too soon.

LORENZO   My brother weeps.
                  All Florence mourns, and little wonder, for
                  She was adorned with every human grace.
                  Beauty, in death's unearthly radiance,
                  Excels, reflected in our flashing grief.
                  Look! Evening's star sky-rides with a new splendour!
                  Her soul has climbed up high where angels dance.
                  Lead the procession now to All Saints' Church,
                  Where, in their vault, Vespucci ancestors
                  Will welcome her slight movement in their dust;
                  And all, tomorrow, come to our Cathedral.
                  There, under the Dome, Rome's Cardinal
                  The seventeen-year-old Raffaello
                  Riario, new-come, will celebrate
                  High Requiem Mass for Simonetta's soul.

                  SIMONETTA'*s body is taken off. It must not be
                  on-stage for the following scene.*

SCENE FOURTEEN

Dim lights to indicate a day passes.
Lights up. Music of Choralis Constantinus by Hein-
rich Isaac. Full crowds going into High Mass.
FRANCESCO *looks about for* GIULIANO, *who is not*
there. Goes out. Brings him back, hugging him in
friendship—in fact to see whether he is wearing his
hunting-knife, or a protective corslet. GIULIANO
limps, and leans for some support on FRANCESCO.
When the sanctus bell rings for the elevation of the
Host, FRANCESCO *gives an obvious signal, raises his*
sword, and brings it down on the middle of
GIULIANO'*s head while he is praying. At the same*
time two priests, Maffei and Bagnone, attack
LORENZO. LORENZO *reacts quickly, whirling his*
cloak round, thus deflecting their knives, suffering
only a slight neck wound. One of his bodyguards is
killed (Francesco Nori). LORENZO *leaps away, with*
ANGELO POLIZIANO, *and the scene ends in riot.*
Short blackout, with continual crowd noises of riot.

CROWD   Lorenzo! Lorenzo! Lorenzo! Lorenzo! Lorenzo!

LORENZO appears on balcony; white, neck
bandaged.

LORENZO   My people; give me leave to speak! Control
                   Yourselves. Let justice take its course.
                   My wound is slight, not serious . . .

His speech is drowned in cheering and applause.

FRANCESCO *is pulled before him.*

Indoor scene; LORENZO *has turned in from the balcony.*

LORENZO   Why have you done this?

FRANCESCO   For our Father in God
Sixtus, in Rome; for all who cannot bear
Two young men turned to eagles, who have raped
The heart of the Republic with their charm,
Money, skilled influence, and patronage.

LORENZO   You killed my brother. They say nineteen wounds
Were found dug in his body. Take him and hang
          him
From a high window in the city palace!

Maffei and Bagnone are pushed to him.

Maffei and Bagnone; you two—priests!—
Tried to kill me. God turned aside your thrusts.
Cut off their ears and noses, and then hang
Them above the Piazza della Signoria.

They are removed to execution.

Sandro?

SANDRO   Magnificence?

LORENZO   Forty gold florins
Are yours. Paint each of the conspirators
In portrait frescoes on the public walls
Of Prison and Grand Brothel; and beneath
Lines, epitaphs, that I shall write on them
For all to see.

SANDRO *retires.* LORENZO *on balcony again.*

                        The Priors have decreed
All Pazzi coats of arms shall be destroyed

Throughout this city. Their property is now
Confiscated; palaces, stables, all
Down to the poultry and the household pans,
Tossed to your public auction. Whoever marries
Any descendant of Andrea de' Pazzi
Shall lose his rights to public office. Now
A medal shall be struck, given free to all
Who stood by us in our calamity.

Applause. LORENZO *turns indoors.*

SCENE SIXTEEN

DOMENICO   Magnificence, the passions of us all
Are scorpioned to bare our blades for you.
My father, Tommaso, whose golden flowers
Garland the head of every girl in Florence,
My brothers David, and lame Benedetto,
And every citizen the lily breeds,
Pain for you in your grief. The youngest knows
That violence must have its echo, tears;
And tears half-dry with shared compassion's touch.
Three girls outside, with life picked from the fields,
Ask leave to lay their pity at your feet.

LORENZO   (*Looking out of the window at mob*)
We must restrain, hold back our active friends.
Forgiveness, too, is tragic, as it springs
From heartbreak; we are men, not gods: but thanks,
To you, and all. Yes! Let kind beauty in.

Enter MARIETTA, ALBIERA, SALVESTRA; FICINO
behind.

MARIETTA   Lilies, blossom of Medici oranges;

ALBIERA   Anemones for short-lived happiness;

SALVESTRA   And violets, the tears of Lent, for grief;

MARIETTA   These April gifts increasing day exchanges

ALBIERA   For Winter's dark and seeming endlessness.

SALVESTRA   Brief was the cornflower crown in laurel leaf.

LORENZO   All things that grow upon the fruitful earth
               Must die. The uncontainable's enclosed.
               Those aspirations are confined, foreclosed,
               That brighten and idealize our birth.
               The furthest reaches naked thought, in mirth,
               Explores round circling heaven, or hell exposed,
               Creation's joy, all that we had supposed
               Possible, lies in soil—one sunflower's worth.

DOMENICO   Leave, leave; he feels the damp upon his heart.

LORENZO   Thanks, graceful friends : forgive me if we part.

                    SCENE SEVENTEEN

               LORENZO *and* FICINO.

FICINO   You need to rest and think of other things
               Awhile. Come to this window, now, and see
               The Tuscan roofs against a cloud-blue sky.

LORENZO   Tiny birds chirrup in the olive trees
               Whose leaves, dark underneath, part to the sky,
               Sun-drenched. Far children's voices call on the air
               Scattered, unleashed from school. Yet there are some
               Who hoped that I would never hear or see
               Such things, or even my own family;
               The startling beauty of a hawk in flight,
               The scent of grain and apples in a barn . . .

FICINO   Such sense-impressions reach the soul through doors
               And windows of the body, our fine senses,
               Stamp our imagination with their image
               Which we compare with our innate ideas,
               And judge, for better or for worse, to be

Beautiful, true, or wise; veiled in birth-dreams,
Dawning self-wakening finds what we know.

Enter DOMENICO.

DOMENICO Lorenzo. May your Sandro bring to you
Something to gladden and dissolve a little
The millstone round your heart?

LORENZO   A painting?

DOMENICO   Yes.

LORENZO Fetch Giorgio Vespucci; Angelo;
Bring in the girls that gave these loving flowers.
My appetite for beauty must not fade,
Blow out, or gutter low.

FICINO   Art nurtures faith.

LORENZO Sandro knows, so well, how to quicken my
Vision of all-creating life; can help
Sadness to see with fresher eyes still young.

They enter.

Come! Each sit down! What painting do you
  bring?

SANDRO Ficino's dream; your challenge to my brush;
A picture for your own Academy
On the green slopes of Montevecchio.

He shows his painting 'Primavera'.

Calm Venus, mother of life's harmony,
Presides, virtuous, clothed. The rest is yours.

LORENZO Show on! Show on! No! We'll discuss it first—
Guess at its secret doctrine, and then you
Correct and guide us. Ah! What ravishing

Beauty of form! Solemn, and classical;
Yet, in expression, Florentine, bizarre,
Modern, fantastic with invention's grace.

DOMENICO   The colours do not fight the perfect line,
But are subdued, enhancing a wild skill.

LORENZO   Poliziano! Can you read the myth?

POLIZIANO   Yes, Ovid tells how Zephyr, the spring wind,
Breathed, seized on Chloris—nymph all winter-
bare—
And turned her into Spring. 'I who was Chloris
Now am called Flora.'

SANDRO   Yes. The year's new bride.

LORENZO   Giorgio Vespucci: what of the dancing three?

VESPUCCI   The same reversed: that Grace who turns her back,
Chastity, moves towards Voluptuousness,
Drawing sweet Married Love round after her.

LORENZO   Marsilio Ficino! Come. The thought!

FICINO   Grace in giving, accepting, returning, while
Placed palm to palm, and interlocked, they lift
The crowned knot of the dance. Once more we see
Descent, Rapture, Return; front, back, and side;
A metamorphosis of love unfolds
In Venus' garden. Fructified in time
By passion's breath, we grow, dance, then return
To heaven, like Mercury, in contemplation,
Prayer reaching up to move aside the clouds
That shield us from the scorching light of God.

LORENZO   Cupid then fires his dart at Chastity
And drives the circle of our passions round?
Domenico; you know your friend. Tell all!

DOMENICO   I recognize the cupid; so will you.

It is a homage from the holy tomb
Of the Medici, done by Donatello
In the Old Sacristy of San Lorenzo.

LORENZO   Sandro, you pay the perfect compliment!

DOMENICO   Unvarnished tempera on a gesso ground . . .
Flora's distilled from his old tutor's panel
'The Birth of John the Baptist', which Antonio
Pallaiuoli made for the Baptistry.

LORENZO   Perhaps his draughtsmanship is as you say,
But Filippo Lippi's sweetness sings to me.
Doesn't that bush of myrtle flecked in white
Seem like a halo round Queen Venus' head?
And look beyond the orange grove. The scene
Stretches far off into serenity.

FICINO   The structure of the whole's in every part,
Sandro; yet there's one thing I cannot see
Or understand. Where's the third group of three?

SANDRO   Mercury points up. Where would you expect?

VESPUCCI   Above, out of the picture!

SANDRO   Yes. No man
Can paint the Holy Christian Trinity
Of which our triads in this life below
Are glass-stained imitations.

LORENZO   Blessed be God!
Ripe fruit, our Tuscan flowers, blossom, trees,
And naked beauty dancing in a round;
Urgency filling creation; and . . . my brother!
Wings on his sandals, quietly reaching high.
Sandro, you have excelled the highest art.
Classical beauty, Christian harmony,
The Old World and the New, join, blessed by Love.
Teach us your thought.

SANDRO   **Well**; pretty down to earth.
Your brother, yes; and Simonetta's there—
Scatters tight roses from her dress-held lap.
I spend my idle hours, as well you know,
Walking the streets, sketching the passers-by.
Those soft, diaphanous Graces you see dance
Are sitting by you; gentle friends of mine :
Salvestra, Marietta, Albiera.
Look hard; and see Clarice there presiding—
The mother of your children and your wife.

DOMENICO   And who is Chloris? Tell, now. Please don't blush!

SANDRO   Er . . . just a lady from the city square
Called Riguardata.

FICINO   Zephyrus is you!

SANDRO   I paint self-portraits on the right-hand side
At times; if I feel moved.

POLIZIANO   Cupid's my pupil!
Your little son, Piero!

LORENZO   All are there!
'Dawning self-wakening finds what we know'
Indeed, Ficino; eyes now seem more clear.
I, too, like Mercury, will turn away
In meditation on my brother's death
To pray, and be alone. But you must stay—
Each loved one; all. You are my guests today!

END OF ACT ONE

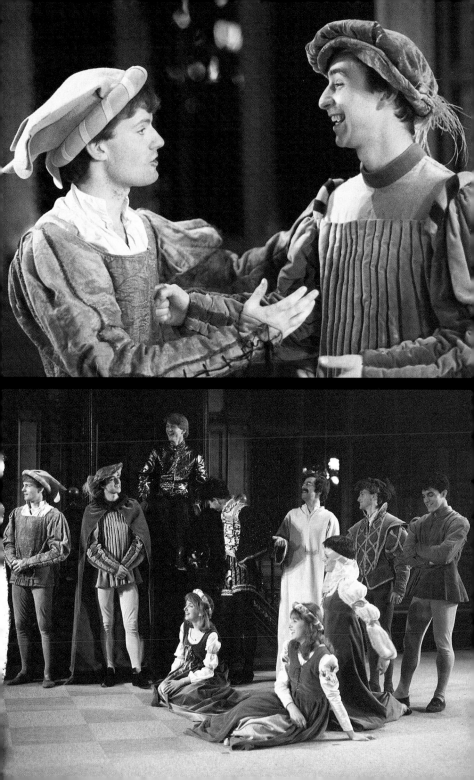

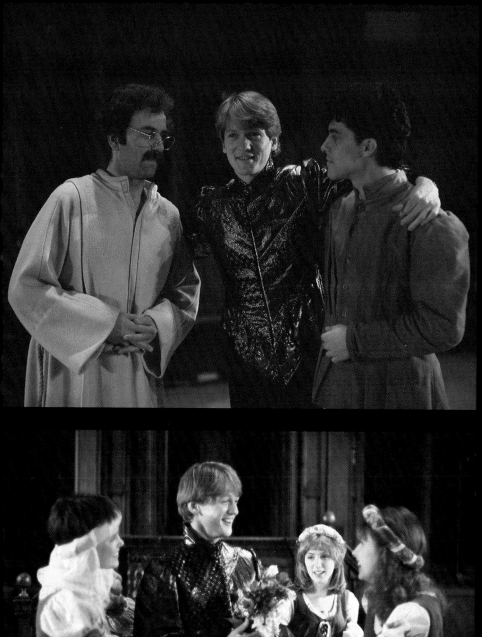

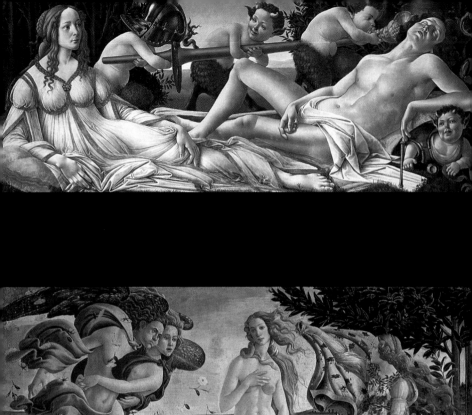

Act Two

PROLOGUES

CLOTHO

I have my hand upon the pulse of life :
One half the thread is spun. No spring returns
For man, or nature; and new buds begun,
Rife in fecundity, must take their turn.
Yes, we three Fates unfold our Mother's law—
Necessity breeds consequence from acts—
Even as three Graces' light timidity
Can pour the love of Venus in our hearts.
Each god, though one, reveals himself in three.
Prosperity can only find fresh flower
When Reason, our soul's charioteer, can be
True master of both horses, black and white :
One, Aspiration; striving for the sky,
To balance black Desire, each held controlled.

LACHESIS

Store this : the gods are not responsible
For free choice man makes in stupidity.
Lucidity is all. If there is fault,
The chooser bears that freedom evermore.
Strife alternates with harmony. Lorenzo
Was three when Rome's long empire, overrun
Under the dome of Constantinople, fell
To the young Máhomet the Second's knife.
High springtime yields to summer, then to age.
Our second act follows the story through
Dying Lorenzo's life-work thrown to waste,
Squandered by Savonarola's piety.
She who allots now takes her leave of you,
And begs you think of your posterity.

SCENE ONE

SALVESTRA *and* MARIETTA.

SALVESTRA Ah, Marietta, you come dancing in
With all the freshness of a new idea.
Here, take my baby while I tie my hair.

MARIETTA Little Battista, welcome to our world!
And may you be as mild and gentle-hearted
When you command the apothecary's shop
As is your father, Luca.

SALVESTRA   May he be
Better with money! These too cruel wars
Waged by Pope Sixtus with Ferrante of Naples
On us—and why? To make our loved Lorenzo
Apologize for not being killed by Pazzi—
Have raised the price of crushed beans to four lire
A bushel; peas, to five. And now the plague!
Who would have thought that would come back to
Florence?

MARIETTA In the Casa del Capitano, a man
Life-sentenced died of the plague. Another prisoner
Taken to La Scala hospital
From the same cell, spread it. Forty are sick.
The hospital now buries every day
At least eleven.

SALVESTRA   Our troops have taken back
Castelnuovo, but bubonic plague
Breathes through exhausted tents.

MARIETTA   God help us all!

Enter ALBIERA, *running.*

ALBIERA Dearest Salvestra, your pink, shawled-up babe
Must cheer your universe!

SALVESTRA   Yes, Albiera :
He's worth it—though my husband sleeps at work.
Come : are you well? What is the news from
      Naples?

MARIETTA   The wind has not dispelled the mist all day.
Welcome back, Albiera! Can you clear
Our fog of dread with some sunshaft of hope?

ALBIERA   I can! I'm out of breath; my throat sounds like
The creaking door of a grown badger's voice.
That glass of wine—thanks!

SALVESTRA   While you were away,
A man was hanged here; taken down as dead,
But woke up! So they tried to bring him round,
Gave him the kiss of life, carted him to
Santa Maria Nuova hospital;
Nursed him to health two weeks. He vowed revenge,
And criticized the staff : and so the Priors
Decided he should hang a second time
As soon as he was well. This time he was
Successful, and hanged dead.

MARIETTA   Salvestra! Quiet!
She has some news, and you keep prattling on.

SALVESTRA   I'm sorry. Right! My head is full of silence.
(*Feeds her baby*)

ALBIERA   This news I bring's immense, although I'm
                nothing—
A sun-drawn daisy in the pushing grass—
Yet tiny spaces hold the greatest force,
A small spark's a great fire; one seed, a tree.
So, bend your ears into my anecdote
And listen. As you know, Lorenzo went
To King Ferrante, who was once his friend,
Now with the Pope warring against us all.
He left unguarded; wrote the Signoria
A letter from San Miniato. 'I give

Myself into Ferrante's hands, alone.
This war was started in my brother's blood;
If God so wills, let my blood end it all
And Florence find sweet peace. If they still war,
We know their claim that I am all they want
Is mere excuse for plunder.'

MARIETTA   But what happened?
He certainly was brave! When Piccanini,
The Milanese, tried this, with a safe-conduct
To Naples, Ferrante put him in a dungeon
And had his throat blocked.

ALBIERA   Ferrante's son, and grandson,
Welcomed upon the quay embarked Lorenzo.
The king himself was absent, hunting, but
Had, at his own cost, painted and tapestried
Naples' Medici bank for our Lorenzo's
Stay there. And Lorenzo charmed him. Peace
Has come!—with a magnificent white horse,
Finer even than that, twelve years ago,
He gave Lorenzo for Lucrezia's joust.

SALVESTRA   Carnival! Praise God!

MARIETTA   Praise Lorenzo, too.

SCENE TWO

Enter SANDRO *and* DOMENICO.

ALBIERA   Sandro! Domenico! You're back from Rome!
Have you completed all that Sistine Chapel?

DOMENICO   I painted a Resurrection over a door
Which they have rebuilt, ruining my work!

SANDRO   No, no. Really! I think it's much improved.
(DOMENICO *hits* SANDRO)
His 'Christ calling Peter and Andrew from
Their nets' has no hole in it yet.

DOMENICO   Thank God.
There was a penalty of fifty gold
Ducats on any one of us still left
After the Ides of March.

SANDRO   I don't believe
Those crazy walls Sixtus put up too fast
Can stand!

DOMENICO   Then all ten histories in paint,
Taken from both the Testaments, will fall.

ALBIERA   Oh, I can't bear to think of it!

SANDRO   The pay
Was good : so was the life there.

DOMENICO   Not a word!

SALVESTRA   Oh I can guess.

SANDRO   Can you? I've made it breed
A painting for Lorenzo's great return.

SANDRO *shows 'Pallas and the Centaur'.*

It shows pure Pallas powdered with interlaced
Rings set with diamond points, the Medici emblems.
She holds the halberd of security
In her left hand, while in her right she takes
The forelock, opportunity, of Naples
To tame the Centaur, war.

DOMENICO   Tempera on canvas.

ALBIERA   Gold-yellow buskins!

MARIETTA   Typically, her hair's
Dishevelled.

ALBIERA   Surely that sea's the bay of Naples?

DOMENICO
There is the forward tilt you love so much,
And grass in the foreground. What a grand design!

SALVESTRA
I hope the Centaur is not King Ferrante!
He doesn't like his hair pulled.

MARIETTA
                              Look! The robe
Leaf-green over her white dress, olive-crowned!
If only I could have a dress like that.

ALBIERA
I like the brown flesh tints and dusky flanks
Of the man-horse.

DOMENICO
                    Show at the carnival!

MARIETTA
ALBIERA   } Yes! Show! Show! Show!
SALVESTRA

Enter GIORGIO VESPUCCI.

SANDRO
                        Giorgio Vespucci!

VESPUCCI
What a great picture for the reign of peace!
Now that Ottoman Turks have sacked Otranto,
Cruelly sawn in half between two planks
Our good Archbishop in the city square,
Sixtus faces a Muslim Italy
And has been forced to reconcile with us.
Twelve Florentine ambassadors to Rome,
Joined since by my own cousin, Guidantonio—
Who, Sandro, likes your work—have each one been
Touched by the Papal staff as they knelt down
And kissed his feet in homage. Apologies
Are general and vague. The war's been stopped.
Naples is now our friend again. Lorenzo
Triumphant, for we owe the most to him.
His courage and his daring made us safe.

SALVESTRA, ALBIERA, *and* MARIETTA *dance for joy.*

SANDRO
(*Teasing them*) I think they are in love.

VESPUCCI

                                      At Carnival?
Oh! Yes. I see a wild, ox-like, fixed stare,
Three pale and blushing pairs of cheeks . . .

DOMENICO

                                          Deep sighs,
And hesitating speech; arms tossed about;
Complaining; boasts; overpraise; petulance;
Suspicion . . .

SANDRO

                And bare feet.

MARIETTA

                      Oh?

VESPUCCI

                                  Barefoot because
Love does not walk as boldly as he should
In the affairs of life, but is soon hurt;
Can run; feels things minute we cannot see.

SANDRO

Why, love is naked as a pearl within
A shell, thrown by the sea to land.

VESPUCCI

                                  Sandro,
Living next door to you in the Via Nuova,
I cannot help seeing you as you paint.
Share with us all your beauty from the foam
Created for our heartfelt carnival.

MARIETTA

Who was the girl who posed this time?

ALBIERA

                                  Sandro,
You both live not two hundred yards away
From the La Scala hospital! The plague
Seeps round your own front doors!

SALVESTRA

                                No one is safe.

SANDRO

Clear Albiera, thank you for your care
And thoughtfulness. I own no property.
Why, all my life my workshop has been in
My parents' home; now I've two teen-age pupils,
And a boy of eleven, apprentices.

How can I move? My money goes on paints
And canvases

DOMENICO   Drinking, chaos, and food.

SANDRO   And books. Cristoforo Landino's *Dante*.

DOMENICO   You squander and waste working-time on that!

VESPUCCI   Well; you could sail, perhaps, and find the Indies
Like my dear nephew, Amerigo; paint
The monsters and the naked human folk
Who carve existence from strange innocence :
The men with shaved heads cut like a cock's comb,
Walking with always folded arms. The girls,
Bare-breasted, carry their hands dangling down;
Paint foreheads, cheeks, and legs; and, humming,
        sway
Under exotic plants that speak and weave.

Enter FICINO.

Marsilio Ficino!

FICINO   Greetings, all.
Lorenzo comes! Prepare for Carnival.
But first, before the carts and floats arrive,
The pageants drawn by horses, bands, and flags,
I ask you, Giorgio : please would you revise,
Check thoroughly, and comment carefully on
My now complete translation of all Plato
From Greek to Latin?

VESPUCCI   Well, I'll try!

MARIETTA   He comes!

SCENE THREE

Enter LORENZO, *to acclaim; with* POLIZIANO.

LORENZO   Marsilio and Giorgio; and all!
Shrove Tuesday's here within a week—then Lent
When we must all be shriven. But today
Carnival sets the Devil on the fire
And we shall dance, and celebrate our joy
At peace declared. Ten Barbary stallions,
The gift of kings, start from the meadow gate,
Race at full gallop up the Via della Vigna,
The Market, and the Corso, and speed past
To win embroidered banners we present
At Porta alla Croce. Three o'clock!

ALBIERA   I love the pounding of those beating hooves—
Like herring-gulls drumming their feet to bring
The earthworms to the surface, back in Naples.

SALVESTRA   It brings the crowds out, certainly; but—
earthworms?

ALBIERA   They think it's rain, and so come up to mate.

MARIETTA   And the gulls eat them?

SALVESTRA   What a way to go!

LORENZO   The intellect at play, in concentration,
With mastered creativity to spare,
Needs to see round, to decorate, enlarge,
And probe beneath the wistful tale of things,
Ambushing thoughts obliquely, then head-on;
Dive underneath, or view all from the clouds.
Yes! Ridicule the Devil! But let all
Trades-guilds, inventors, wool-workers, tailors, each
Elaborate a float, and I will pay
If you will decorate your handiwork
With artistry that makes the world aghast.

POLIZIANO
A riot of carts and floats—the scrap-iron dealers,
The millers and the bakers and the cooks,
And cavalcades ambassadorial
Each with a banner, song, and choristers,
Staged Bible-triumphs, and proud mock-
    brigades—
Not least Lorenzo's Company of the Star . . .

ALBIERA
Mighty Lorenzo, may we have new songs
Written by you?

LORENZO
            Spider-down cheeks, you may.
(*To the three girls*)
Let all the scent of music fill your veins.

MARIETTA
Lorenzo; what's the Company of the Star?

LORENZO
A fresh creation to unite all parts
Of Florence, not each neighbourhood alone;
The young, the rich, the poor; each knot's untied
Under the Star of Venus. Dearest Sandro,
Is our commission finished? May we see it?

SANDRO
(*Starting to unpack picture*)
Heaven's but the vision of fulfilled desire,
And Hell the shadow of a soul on fire
Cast on the darkness into which ourselves,
So late emerged from, shall so soon expire.

DOMENICO
Whatever do you mean? Magnificence,
Bear with him. He's been eating roses and
The thorn's stuck in his teeth.

LORENZO
               Perhaps we'll learn.
Now that I'm older, tomorrow comes more quickly
Than once it did in airy silvered youth
When time stayed like gauze dust on a moth's wing
Trembling the sun. My Sandro, is it done?
Come! Show your stellar celebration here.

SALVESTRA
Ah! Shall we see it?

MARIETTA

Yes! But who stood naked?
I'll recognize her.

ALBIERA

Oh, I'm so excited!
Every few moments I get a cold shudder
All down my back; you know, like overhearing
Confession in the dark.

LORENZO

Oh give me friends
And not admirers—people like yourselves.
Sandro, God knows how much I appreciate
Judgement; how little I care for opinion.
Unveil the morning star!

SANDRO *unveils 'The Birth of Venus'.*

What an unutterable sense of loss:
It's Simonetta!

MARIETTA

From so long ago.

SALVESTRA

Oh, she brings back my teen-age youth, that world
Of whispered secrets and spontaneous hugs,
A hand squeezed, unexpected; and the blatant
Sudden fresh kiss in a shop doorway.

ALBIERA

Yes;
Love is the best thing that there is: unspeakably
Precious; and whatever captures it
Shares in that preciousness.

DOMENICO

Sandro; my God,
You've done it!

FICINO

Yes, you have. This kind of glow
Does not descend into our earthly matter
Until the matter has been well prepared,
And brush, mind, soul, emotions, pearl in one.

DOMENICO

This you could not have painted before Rome.

VESPUCCI   Puffing cut roses . . . what are those gales of passion?

LORENZO   Grief; grief. It is incomparable. Your best.
Thank you; just thanks.

SANDRO   It was your Angelo
Who gave the theme : his verses on the joust
For Giuliano.

LORENZO   Say them now, my poet.

POLIZIANO   A naked woman with an angel's face
Blown on a shell, wafted toward the shore
By Zephyrs to where Hours with loosened pace
Welcome her like a sister, and restore
Her modesty with Nature's endless grace
Of flowers. Her soft loveliness must awe
Those who look on. Her *left* hand crossed one
        breast;
Her other held her long hair where was best.

LORENZO   A duet danced between two sister arts,
Painting and Poetry.

DOMENICO   I can't wait to see
How you have done it. Now, this one's on canvas :
Two strips, and sewn together all along.

SANDRO   All that I could get hold of at the time.

DOMENICO   The yolk and viscid glair of egg; low, grassy
Foreground dunes, a forward tilt . . .

POLIZIANO   Medici
Orange trees in flower . . .

LORENZO   Free use of gold
Heightening the lights. Sandro, here radiates
Something that far transcends our Carnival
To speak for Florence and this golden age
Of peace in Tuscany to worlds unwept.

Venus pudica anadyomene
That once Apelles dreamed. Ah, Simonetta!
How strange those lovely syllables feel starved.
Wounded emotions often are unhealed
Memory reaching out for lost relief.
Our lives need more than self, for there must be
A clear, still centre to intensity,
And you have found it.

FICINO   Beauty is divine.
We worship God in things he has created
So we can later worship things in God.
At one with our own innocent Idea
We reach full life, and seem in loving God
To love ourselves.

LORENZO   Here's a farewell to flesh :
Carne, vale! Sing it while I leave
To find my wife, Clarice.

MARIETTA   SONG

I am my own delight, new in the spring
    Of maidenhood, to give to whom I choose,
And in my mirror I find everything
        That brings contentment. Yes! One day I'll
        lose
The bird-song freshness of this cloud-pink cheek—
But now my flower and blossom is unique.

And as I look about me as I walk
    At all the colours that wave up at me,
Bright-scented laughter, each one on its stalk
        Proud in its one day's glory, just to be;
I wink back in my mirror, and decide
No man on earth shall take me as his bride.

SCENE FOUR

CLARICE *and* POLIZIANO.

CLARICE

Oh, where have you been leading him?

POLIZIANO

Clarice,
Six floats have been prepared with stage sets, built
In image to depict the Life of Christ.

CLARICE

Yes, so they should; and always have : but now
Beside the Bible stories, other carts
And carriages present our family.
It is not right. Orsini up in Rome
Never allow the fair-ground in their home,
Nor let crude actors strut before the crowds
Dressed as ourselves!

POLIZIANO

Madonna; just this once,
To praise Lorenzo, all the city votes
To show its gratitude. You should be proud!
The caravan of pageants shows the Roman
Consul Aemilius Paulus coming home
In triumph with such wealth no Roman paid
Taxes for fifty years, thanks to his conquests.

CLARICE

Well, that was ancient Rome. Today, tomorrow,
Taxes must still be paid—we pay too much!
And though Lorenzo has indeed brought peace
For Florence, he has lost it in himself;
Cannot relax; is ill; writes wanton songs
And endlessly encourages his guild,
The Star . . .

POLIZIANO

To bring together rival groups
In this fragmented, layered community.
What wrong is that?

CLARICE

What! Men like Doffo Spini?

POLIZIANO   This city, now so unified by war
             And sudden peace, could split in two without
             The benediction of your husband's touch.
             Thank all the gods on high!

CLARICE   Now, that's what's wrong!
             You, an ecclesiastic, think much more
             Of Virgil, Plato, and God knows what pagans
             Else, when you should teach my son of Christ!
             Oh, what this city needs is a new spirit
             Far from the nakedness and revelry,
             The painted harlots, and the monks with lutes,
             Lascivious wives and daughters out in search
             Of eyes that flatter, and the tickling tongue,
             To turn us back to sanctity and God.
             Isn't cold Aphrodite on your mind
             Far more than ever is our Virgin Mary?

POLIZIANO   I teach Piero both the word of God
             And style of Cicero. I have no fear
             He will not master learning in good time
             And fulfil all that you expect of him.

CLARICE   Don't you presume your claim upon my husband
             Entitles you to mock me with grave words!
             I have endured a thousand insults here
             No one would show in Rome to an Orsini—
             And everything you do, your books, Academy,
             Sever him from my side. Those hateful Greeks
             Loved women far less often than young men.
             Oh I could scream!   (*Exit*)

POLIZIANO   Welcome outstayed is worse than a bad dream.
             (*Exit*)

SCENE FIVE

SALVESTRA, ALBIERA, MARIETTA.

SALVESTRA   These shows on carts are very daring!

ALBIERA   Well,
I should feel cold, like that!

SALVESTRA   Look! Spiritegli
High on their stilts walk above heads, on air!

MARIETTA   And giants with huge poles for walking-sticks!

ALBIERA   No, they're not giants—they are on stilts, too!
What hideous masks!

MARIETTA   There goes the Devil, masked; forked tail, and
horns!

SALVESTRA   Belching out sulphur from his elephant nose . . .

ALBIERA   Hurray! He's chased by a fat monk who beats
His padded bottom with a heavy stick!

SALVESTRA   The crowd's wild with delight! Now to the fire
To burn the Devil in our city square.   (*Exeunt*)

SCENE SIX

VESPUCCI *and* LORENZO.

VESPUCCI   Seize the time.
Now winds of luck fill out your driving sails
To speed the craft of state under your hand,
Reshape the sea in which you sail—with care,
Anything you suggest will be allowed.
Ask the Signoria, who each are yours,
To choose a group of thirty Florentines,

And then co-opt up to the number seventy.
Concentrate power in this new-formed group—
Broad-based, but yours—and make it permanent.

LORENZO   Repeatable certainties that last make rule
Sweeter, and more efficient; but just say
They fell in the wrong hands? Look : I grow
lame . . .

Enter CLARICE.

CLARICE   The infinite and spacey air of night
Breezes upon our cheeks; come, can you rest?

Enter POLIZIANO.

POLIZIANO   Ah, dear Lorenzo; Florence owes its riches
To you who make it wealthy, safe for thought.

LORENZO   Thank you. Clarice asks a special favour.
I thought we had enough monks in this place,
But both she, and your friend Count Mirandola,
Speak of Fra Girolamo from Ferrara.
What do you say about inviting him
To our Dominican monastery here,
San Marco, so loved by my grandfather?

POLIZIANO   Pico admires him.

CLARICE   And does my word count?

LORENZO   Right! We shall invite, if he cares to accept,
Fra Girolamo to San Marco's garden,
Where he may preach and read. There he shall live
In quiet, and in prayer for us all.
Now, you two : heal sad wounds. Kiss; be at peace.

CLARICE *and* POLIZIANO *embrace.*

My mother's died; the perfect counsellor :
And leaves a void that never can be filled.

Dim lights briefly.

SCENE SEVEN

SALVESTRA, ALBIERA, MARIETTA. *Enter to them*
SAVONAROLA.

SAVONAROLA You sing these songs and strain your lips and eyes
Like two young lovers trying to kiss across
A river; but such thoughts lead you astray.

MARIETTA Are you Fra Girolamo, whom Lorenzo
Called to enhance his monastery here?

SAVONAROLA Savonarola is indeed my name;
But I have come called by the word of Christ
As Prior to San Marco; not by man.

MARIETTA Lorenzo's single gesture bends all wills,
Though he does not abuse his mastery.

ALBIERA They say you are austere; but have you been
In love?

SALVESTRA Oh, Albiera! What a question!

SAVONAROLA I played the lute; and still I love its sounds
For holy words. Yes, daughter. Long ago,
Facing my parents' home across the street
In old Ferrara, came a family
Exiled from Florence for opposing your
Medici: yes, you've guessed: the Strozzi clan.
Roberto Strozzi's daughter with dark eyes
Stared at me from the window opposite
As I was shaving—those winding streets are
      narrow—
And there she was, so close we nearly touched.
I fell in love. We walked. A servant whispered
To me that she was illegitimate.
Imagine my disgust! I fought it down,
Obsessively in love: forgave her all!
Even the fact her mother was not hers!

Two months I wrote a letter every day;
Composed her songs: Laudomia's silken hair!
She never wrote back, but we now linked hands
And laughed, held buttercups under our chins
To find each other's tastes. I bought new clothes
Gorgeous as those St. Francis shrugged before
He ran to God. One day, high on Ferrara's
Ramparts, the air was soft. I played her song.
Laudomia smiled, and looked so beautiful
I asked her to marry me. She froze in pride;
And said the noble Strozzi could not think
Of marriage with the lower Savonarolas,
Grandchildren of a doctor! From that day
I've never looked upon a woman's face
With joy.

MARIETTA   Don't judge all women by just one.
We have our faults, God knows! But you are here
To teach us how forgiveness comes from God.
The deepest sickness is the spiritual.
How can you bless us if you hate us so?

SAVONAROLA   No hatred, daughter. I speak of long-past,
Far-distant days, before my vows were locked,
When this world seemed attractive, now no more
In its sucked sweetmeat decadence and sin
Than a dead horse strawed in a stable yard.

Enter POLIZIANO.

POLIZIANO   Fra Girolamo, welcome! Have you heard
The new Pope, Innocent the Eighth, has given
His son to be Lorenzo's daughter's spouse?
And what is more, Lorenzo's second son
Giovanni is made a Cardinal at thirteen!

SAVONAROLA   See! The world turns to chaos. Virtue, goodness,
Spin into darkness, while triumphant Pride
Glories in rape and feeds on kindred's blood,
Riding the Chair of Rome like men at tilt.

Blest are all those who force the widows' tears.
Gentle and beautiful of soul is he
Who wins, by violence and fraud, the scorn
Of heaven, and tramples down cries of despair.

POLIZIANO   You must not speak like this. His Holiness
Is ill to death; only survives by drinking
Women's milk.

SAVONAROLA   I prophesy three deaths
In high place, and a scourge to carnival
Sweeping away the tinsel that deforms
Great Dante's city, here. Down from the Alps
The fire of God will cleanse his holy place,
Beat at the doors of Florence, then swirl on
Riding the rivers to Eternal Rome
In unencounterable ecstasy.

POLIZIANO   Have you quite finished? Look : Lorenzo's ill;
And hopes you'll pay the customary visit
Each Prior's made since our Saint Antonino
Courtesied great Cosimo, who endowed
The beauty Fra Angelico enhanced.

SAVONAROLA   A finger writes upon Belshazzar's wall :
'God has weighed your kingdom : found it wanting.
The Medes and Persians shall divide the spoil.'

SCENE EIGHT

LORENZO *and* FICINO.

LORENZO   The sky's bleak icy breath inflames my gout,
Our family's disease. Perhaps my love
Of beauty, action, hunting, and good friends
Presents its price?

FICINO   Respect vitality.
We know our Saviour joins himself to man
Directly; what must follow then is man

Can reach for God through his God-given senses.
Honey is the best friend sick people have;
Fresh cheese, sweet apples, betany, and figs.
But those who eat should sit among the pines
To inhale their scent; or lie beneath a vine;
And rub the body with oil from those trees.
Mix with young, carefree people who are healthy,
And—not too much diversity of food.

Enter POLIZIANO.

POLIZIANO Lorenzo, our grim friar is circumspect;
I might say obstinate. You have invited
The sly Dominican to preach the Lent
Sermons. With veiled ambiguity
He prophesies your death; the Pope's; Ferrante's.
A scourge will flay across the Alps, he warns;
And long-eared donkeys listen to his tales.

LORENZO Men are not perfect, and those things are best
Which cause least evil. Prophecy is one.
If men can be restrained by fears foreseen
We can avoid the worst. If idle words
Strike fear into a gaping congregation
That now is here and now is gone, what harm
Provided he does not subvert the state?

POLIZIANO May I, to counteract Cassandra's voice,
Gold-leaf inside the chapel of the gorgeous
Villa Lemmi a homage to your mother?
'Giovanni Tornabuoni here has caused
Poliziano to inscribe this date,
The year of Our Lord Fourteen Ninety, when
Our noble city, beautied by her wealth,
Her victories, her arts, her mighty buildings,
Glories in plenty, health, and tranquil peace.'

LORENZO Yes, do. And tell Girolamo, the interests
Of the Medici house are one with Florence.
Look! Dear Ficino has completed all
Plotinus now, as well as Plato! Since

Constantinople fell, no place on earth
Can match our springtime rebirth of old learning
And new thought. Pico is here! Manuscripts come!

FICINO

Savonarola's grandfather, who taught
Our grim-browed Prior as a boy, wrote strange
Textbooks on women's gynaecology.

POLIZIANO

No wonder his distorted view of life
Lingers on sins that Jesus Christ forgave.
Why, he condemns your poems; Petrarch's; all
The words of nurtured memory and fun.

LORENZO

The young must dance, the life-force be respected,
And sprigs of energy must push beyond
Mere branches of past opportunity
If the great cycle of the ages is
To bear its fruit. Tell him my recent verses
Are meant for God who guarantees all meaning.
Though we may mock, I believe he's sincere
And incorruptible—that's rare, these days.
A stranger's come into my house : I hope
That he will deign to visit me?

POLIZIANO

We'll see.

SCENE NINE

SANDRO *and* DOMENICO.

DOMENICO

All right! We disagree. That man is evil :
An enemy to beauty and to God!

SANDRO

But say he's right?

Enter SAVONAROLA.

SAVONAROLA

Look steadily at life!
You two have power to lead the eye astray,
Domenico and Sandro—image-makers.

Look, mothers! how you trick up your fresh girls
As nymphs brought out to parade this Cathedral
And taunt men's eyes on cattle-market day.
You are the idols in the sanctuary!
We kneel down to a painting on the wall
Behind the altar : there's the Magdalen.
Whose face? Why, that of a notorious whore!
When did the Virgin Mary dress in robes
Loaned by Medici? Saint John has the outline
Of a fat banker, or known catamite.
You put your scholars in among the saints,
And Holy Women show unholy breasts,
Known features recognizable to all
In Florence, to our scandal and disgrace!
I call a curse on nudity today,
Whatever form or shape—statue, or glass,
Goldwork or ceiling—it may contaminate.
Lascivious pictures lead to amorous thoughts,
Thoughts on to actions, actions toss to Hell!

Climbs into pulpit.

An inward fire consumes my fasting bones
Compelling me to speak. Lord! What reward
Shall there be waiting in the life to come
For those who triumph on this battlefield?
Great ladies beg the brothels should be closed.
What? Are you jealous? But I say to you
Fat kine of Bashan who oppress the poor,
First take the jewelled beam out of your eye!
Your wanton, proud extravagance of clothes,
Your faces rubbed with paint, your charcoaled eyes,
Your dyed hairs, opened arms, seek to ensnare
Priests and young monks in love-nests, poisoned, perfumed
Houses of sin. The prostitutes are poor :
They imitate their betters. Know yourselves!
I shall decree, though, that no street-walking,
Soliciting from doors or balconies,
May be allowed in Lent (with the exception
Of mid-Lent Mardi Gras). Gambling is rife!

Fathers teach sons, mothers their daughters, too!
This city is not Florence, but a den
Of thieves. Look round, and see how avarice grows!
Usury's whirlpool widens. Lust contaminates
All things. Pride soars up to crowd the clouds.
The saying of Isaiah is fulfilled :
'They sin as Sodom and they hide it not.'
Yes! Sodomy is the destructive scourge
Of Florence! Parents, teachers, you're to blame.
You smile : 'The boys should find rich, older men
Who'll save our purse, and pay their education.
Besides, there are no awkward pregnancies.'
Mothers, I beg you : do not send your boys
On errands. Let the girls go out instead;
They are less vulnerable to this vice.
And yet the Devil's hatchet's soon at work :
A girl walks modestly, is well brought up,
The axe of flattery is at her root
And fells her virtue. I am the plague of hail
That pelts on all who walk the open air!
Lay off your green and yellow spectacles,
Envy and Passion. Wear the transparent glass
Of Mercy and of Truth. You build your city
On a whale's back. Soon it will plunge, and all
The sky-touched edifices will dissolve
Beneath the waves of time. Babylon is
Destroyed. And yet, today, I say to you
Florence can be the New Jerusalem,
Destined inheritor of mighty Rome!
You behold light and darkness, and prefer
The carnivals of night. Proud tyrants rule
Lacquered in flattery. They sap the poor,
Corrupt the voters, and keep dubious gains.
You must not imitate them! Come! Bring here
Your amorous poems, lecherous nudities,
Your song-books, ballads, chess-boards, playing-
        cards,
Your wigs and mirrors, musical instruments,
Ivories, alabaster games, and all
Tapestries showing wanton pagan scenes.
Pile on this pyramid, sixty feet high,

All these immodesties that wall you out
From Heaven, hold back Florence from her high
Destiny as the city ruled by Christ!
Throw! Let the fire flame blaze!

*Burning of the Vanities, church bell ringing, and
storm drenching all, ended by thunder.*

SCENE TEN

DOFFO SPINI   This man lacks any civilizing taste
Or style. He's sex-obsessed; preposterous;
And bad for trade.

SANDRO   Perhaps he is sincere?

DOFFO SPINI   Sincere? He hates mankind—arts, learning, all
That cannot be reduced to penitence
And ashes. He looks at his crucifix
And cries: 'If I lie, Jesus, so do you!'

SANDRO   That may be his belief.

DOFFO SPINI   He should believe
Indoors, then, and alone; hygienically.
Friaries are houses for those with character
Deficiencies; that's why they are locked in
At night, and only let out on parole.
Look; Sforza of Milan, and Caterina—
Lady of Imola and Forli—want him
Silenced. Lorenzo is too ill to see
The danger on his doorstep, and too generous
To stifle criticism. Come tonight
And dine with thirty Compagnacci boys.
There are three hundred of us who have sworn
To bring this philistine psalm-singer into
Focus—perhaps with a burning-glass.
The Pitti Palace, once the sun's gone down!

SANDRO   Doffo Spini, you are, and have been, welcome

In my workshop, and many lively hours
We've drunk away, squashing food into paints.
You know, too, I am slow to take up sides,
Though loyal once I have. Please give me time
To learn more of this man.

DOFFO SPINI He splits the city:
My Compagnacci on the side of life
And pleasure, arts, air, music, and the young,
And these Frateschi on the other side
Hid in Dominican robes, old, loathing all
That adds a colour to the cheeks of girls:
Grey hypocrites who bleat eternal Lent,
And forget Christ was once a wedding-guest.
You know where you will find us? (*Leaving*)

SANDRO Pitti Palace,
Once the great sun's declined.

SCENE ELEVEN

Enter DOMENICO.

Domenico!

DOMENICO While the world gapes with mouths that splutter
gossip
About the 'Good Companions' or 'Psalm-singers',
I have been sketching. Here Vespucci comes.

Enter VESPUCCI.

Ah, Giorgio! I have taken up your hint.
Have you a moment to look at these sketches
Of Amerigo sailing to the Indies?
My last work on an arch was wrecked by papal
Builders. I'll celebrate your timeless nephew
In an unusual misericordia
Over an arch in your Vespucci chapel.

VESPUCCI   (*Glances at sketches*)
                  I was his uncle, tutor, and his friend.
                  Some misericordia! Well, I suppose
                  God's tolerant. Show me another time.
                  Lorenzo's wife, Clarice, has just died.

SANDRO   Has he been told?

VESPUCCI   Not yet. He's gravely ill;
                  And at Filetta in a sad attempt
                  To ease the pain continual he feels,
                  Rests in seclusion with his doctors' skills.
                  The plague is everywhere. Grown, healthy men
                  Drop into darkness over lunch.

DOMENICO   I hope
                  He's well enough to see the outline sketches
                  That I have done for his boy Cardinal
                  At San Giusto Abbey. Well, I am tired.
                  When you have time, and this heart-breaking news
                  Of thirty-five-year-old Clarice's death
                  Has sunk in, may we talk in paint again?

VESPUCCI   Of course. Are you unwell?

DOMENICO   No. I suppose
                  Just shocked. I'm forty-four, a little older
                  Than dear Lorenzo. Three-score years and ten?
                  Which of us stretches to that age these days?

SANDRO   Go and lie down. I'll sketch, then visit you.

                  Exit DOMENICO.

                  Giorgio; you now live within San Marco:
                  Tell me the truth about your Prior.

VESPUCCI   Just this:
                  His strange soul has a grandeur, and a vision
                  Not one of us has ever seen before,
                  Nor will again. His purposes are few,
                  But they are God's.

SANDRO   Thank you. I thought so, too.

Exit VESPUCCI. SANDRO *sketches.*

SCENE TWELVE

Enter SALVESTRA, ALBIERA, *and* MARIETTA.

SALVESTRA   Oh, Sandro, Sandro!

SANDRO   Sit! I'll sketch you there
Once more. Why so excited?

MARIETTA   Thunderbolts
And lightning struck the top of the cathedral,
And two of the marble summit balls have crashed—
One in the piazza . . .

SALVESTRA   Towards the Medici Palace!
The other crushed Luca Ranieri's home!

ALBIERA   The city lions, docile in their cage,
Have turned and fought each other to the death.
It's all unheard of!

SANDRO   Look up! A new comet!

SALVESTRA   Dear God; defend us all!

ALBIERA   Amen.

MARIETTA   Amen.

Blackout.

SCENE THIRTEEN

POLIZIANO *and* SANDRO, LORENZO *dying.*

POLIZIANO   At last, near midnight, his confessor came;
Prepared the Eucharist in the next room.
Lorenzo dragged his trunk up from the couch :
'It must not be my Lord, who made and saved me,
Bends to my chair. I beg you, lift me up
So I may meet him on my knees!' He fell,
Supported by us all, in agony,
And, crying, knelt.
Lorenzo has received viaticum.
Confessed, forgiven, blest, and comforted,
He makes his final journey from this world.

SANDRO   Pico has left; outside, Savonarola
Waits.

POLIZIANO   He's come at last!

SANDRO   Lorenzo asked
For them to be alone before he dies.

POLIZIANO   Is this dark Prior a saint, or does he pick
Kudos, like offal, from a dying man
Later to boast it?

SANDRO   Let us leave the room.

Exeunt. SAVONAROLA *enters.*

SAVONAROLA   Lorenzo.

LORENZO   Prior.

SAVONAROLA   Have you confessed? Been shriven?
Received the Host, God's Body? How did it taste?

LORENZO   As all things do inside a dying mouth,

Even the latch-key to eternity.
Have I your blessing?

SAVONAROLA   God is merciful.
I have three questions. Will you answer them?

LORENZO   The Lord being my helper; yes, I will.

SAVONAROLA   You say the sack of Volterra still haunts
Your conscience.

LORENZO   So it does! Oh God.

SAVONAROLA   It was
Milanese mercenaries, not yourself,
Whose bloodlust burst and could not be controlled.

LORENZO   In penitence for our troops' breaking faith,
I gave that vultured city golden coin;
But it was still my fault so many disarmed,
Trusting, innocent men and women died.

SAVONAROLA   Do you have faith in God?

LORENZO   I do.

SAVONAROLA   He can
Forgive beyond our mental prison boundaries.
Only believe. All things are possible
As you approach our Maker's judgement-seat.
Will you give back, especially to the poor,
The widows' daughters, and the orphaned girls,
Our city's ancient fund for dowry gifts
That this sick State has pilfered?

LORENZO   True. My pain
Has been so great I have neglected, passed
Without full opposition, those sad laws
That snatch young wedding from the lips of love
And force her into poverty and vice.

SAVONAROLA   Will you restore the city's liberties?

LORENZO   Like Cicero, there are two things I wish :
               That I may leave all Florentines in peace
               And liberty, when I discard this corpse;
               And that each citizen may hold the chance
               To help our common good in self-respecting
               Trade or occupation.

               POLIZIANO *and* FICINO *enter.*

                              Come, my friends.
               Yes; there's a third : I wish that creeping death
               Had spared me to complete your libraries.
               My star is setting. No tears. Will you read
               The Last Words of our Lord and Christ to me?

SAVONAROLA   'After this, Jesus knowing that all things were now
               accomplished, that the scripture might be fulfilled,
               saith, "I thirst." Now there was set a vessel full of
               vinegar : and they filled a spunge with vinegar, and
               put it upon hyssop, and put it to his mouth. When
               Jesus therefore had received the vinegar, he said,
               "It is finished" : and he bowed his head, and gave
               up the ghost.'

POLIZIANO   He's still.

FICINO   Here; hold these spectacles, and see . . .
               (*Holds spectacles to* LORENZO'*s mouth*)
               He breathes! His finger beckons . . . a crucifix!
               Yes—kiss it to his lips.

POLIZIANO   His spirit goes;
               He's gone.

               Darkness.

SCENE FOURTEEN

Slow drum. Funeral procession. Funeral music.

POLIZIANO

(*From public balcony*)
Come, pour water on my head,
Give my eyes the fountain's tears
So that I may weep the dead,
Weeping still when morning clears.
So the bereft turtle-dove,
Nightingale, and dying swan,
Mourning loss of earthly love,
Weep as shadowed death creeps on.
Now the laurel fallen lies
After lightning's sudden stroke.
Though the earthly body dies,
And the nymphs and Muses choke
With their sobs of broken grief,
And his tongue's for ever mute,
Yet our hearts must find relief,
Though this world's left destitute
Of the man who held us dear,
Saved our city and our arts :
He has nothing left to fear.
Now he lives on in our hearts.

SANDRO

Now begin the troubles of Italy.

SCENE FIFTEEN

VESPUCCI, SALVESTRA, ALBIERA, MARIETTA.

MARIETTA

What's happening?

VESPUCCI

Pope Innocent, our friend,
Whose eyelids closed each night Lorenzo's thoughts,
Has died, and Borgia now has been elected
Alexander the Sixth.

ALBIERA   A Borgia Pope!

SALVESTRA   What next!

Enter FICINO.

FICINO   The spirit that fused soul to body in
                King Ferrante of Naples now has fled
                Back to its origin : his earth, to earth;
                His soul to God.

VESPUCCI   If God is feeling kind!
                That's why the King of France's standing army,
                Left by his father Louis, treads the Alps!

ALBIERA   Has French King Charles twelve toes upon his
                     feet?—
                And is that why the French-styled shoes are broad?

SALVESTRA   He has a purple birth-mark round one eye.

VESPUCCI   But more important, now Ferrante's dead,
                Charles claims that throne of Naples, telling all
                By proclamation, and words secretive,
                With boast and threat, cajoling in one minute
                Then blustering the next, that he is heir
                Of René, Duke of Anjou and late King
                Of the sad city of Jerusalem.

MARIETTA   He never dared when sly Ferrante lived,
                And our Lorenzo sweetened memory.

FICINO   Charles forms a pact with Lodovico Sforza;
                Has crossed the Alps; will soon be at our gates.

VESPUCCI   And Fra Girolamo claims the French king
                Is 'Chosen of God', his scourge!

FICINO   The Borgia Pope
                Has excommunicated Savonarola.
                The Signoria beg him to retract,
                Letting Fra Girolamo preach again.

SCENE SIXTEEN

Enter DOFFO SPINI.

FICINO What brings you to us? And why do you hate
Dominicans?

DOFFO SPINI I don't. But one of you,
Fra Domenico of San Marco's garden,
Defending his mad Prior, challenged Franciscans
To walk through fire to prove their calumny
Of Savonarola. While you were away,
The pent crowd waited for Domenico
Holding a crucifix, and Savonarola
Carrying high the Host, to test the flames.
Each side delays. Franciscans want the other
To strip, so fire can burn the skin; and both
In fears innumerable find delays,
With superstitions that each crucifix
Is a half-mandrake diabolical,
And such-like cowardly fatuities.
The crowd have turned against him whom they
        loved :
And we have tortured him to find the truth.
His hands were tied behind his back, and he
Was hoisted up by the wrists to twenty feet.
Four times in one hour he was dropped, till both
Arms dislocated at the shoulders, elbows,
And left him dangling inches from the floor.
He now confesses all he preached was lies;
So—he must burn. Come, now, and watch the fun.

FICINO Why, so would anyone confess when racked !

DOFFO SPINI We did some other things as well : quite legal.
Unfortunately, he can scarcely walk.
See ! Here he comes. Look ! They erect a scaffold,
And pile brushwood, all soaked in oil and resin
To make it burn. With him there hang two more
Life-haters, Fra Domenico and Silvestro.

VESPUCCI   It looks so like a crucifixion scene!

DOFFO SPINI   We thought of that, and what the crowd might say,
So one cross-beam's been sawn. Look! All want
        blood!
We ourselves almost feared for our own lives,
Though we are innocent. The heretics
Are strangled one by one, and left to burn.

Sounds of fire. Mob. SAVONAROLA's *execution.*

ALBIERA   The crowd's run wild! Protect us, Father!

SALVESTRA   Save us!

VESPUCCI   The crown worn by Our Lady's statue in
San Marco has been lifted off, and now
Decks a drunk prostitute, who laughs, parading
By. The Friary's defaced. Come, all—
Run to the Palace where we shall be safe.

Exeunt VESPUCCI, FICINO, SALVESTRA, MARIETTA.

SCENE SEVENTEEN

SANDRO   Why did you do it—you, and your companions?

DOFFO SPINI   Ah, Sandro. Do you know, if I had been
Closer acquainted with the burning friar,
I might have been a greater devotee
Than you! Because we are old friends, I'll say
What happened—but you keep it to yourself!
Benozzo Federighi was the cause,
Not I; and if we had released the friar—
Sent him back to San Marco (for the truth
Is, we could find no fault at all in him)—
The predatory mob would soon have sacked
The city, and—God knows!—we should have been,
Each of us, cut in pieces!

Exit DOFFO SPINI.

SCENE EIGHTEEN

SANDRO   Expediency.
Yes; right and wrong concern arithmetic,
But good and evil isolate mankind;
Motive is all. Justice? Convenience!
Oh, what cold killers human beings are
When tenderness of family's forgotten,
The father's love for daughter, friendship's song,
Innocent laughter in the picnic grass,
Chosen possessions on a chimney-piece,
Poetry, and the paradise of books,
Conviviality and gentleness
Of peaceful days' contentment both at work
And playtime's ease. Now a vast sense of loss
Crowds in between my ears, plentiful being
Rotting away in grossest negligence.
A Florentine is like a crucifix
Thrown among devils, also Florentines.
Domenico my friend dies of the plague.
Angelo Poliziano's dead;
With Pico, poisoned. All my world has passed.
(*Slide of 'Magdalen at the Foot of the Cross'*)
And falling shields red-blazoned with a cross
Show the Divine wrath striking down Florence.
An angry angel holds the fox, Deceit,
That spoils all vines of peace, and devils hurl
Brands burning to the earth. Ah, Christ! Look on
Our utter waste of all your loveliness,
And, prostrate, let us cling beneath your feet
With Magdalen.

ALBIERA   Sandro, come. Come with me
To safety. You alone taught me that when
Tragedy comes, some guidance how to cope
With it is also given. Perhaps your friar,
Now at the gates of heaven where angels dance,
Found the strong Angel of the Agony,
In that last fire, was with him to the end.

SANDRO   Gentleness, thank you. Bless you!

ALBIERA   Death is rife.
Officers went into the hospitals
This morning, and drove out all those with plague.
They put a pulley on a rope outside
The Arte de Corazzai, just to hang
Any who might return into the city.
It is a brutal and harsh remedy.

SANDRO   My last sands drop. Here—see my final work.
Other and younger men must now paint on
For the new century, forgetting me.
My friend Domenico's pupil, Michelangelo;
Strange Leonardo; the boy Raphael;
And others that I cannot understand.
For me the stable child at Bethlehem,
(*Slide of 'Mystic Nativity'*)
Hope of the homeless, outcast, and the cold,
Rejected, and the afraid, blows through my
          thoughts,
Stirring my dying brush across the paint.
When the trees' tousled hair rustles with dawn,
And rough ship's rigging's whispered through by
          ghosts
Who whistle in key-holes, moan down chimney-
          breasts,
When the high morning star has banished night,
Unveiling all the brightness of new day,
The East wind falls, and streaked clouds hint of
          rain,
And shells, those varied footprints of the waves,
Scatter across the sprawled and beaten sand,
See, there is nothing left unshakeable,
Solid, or lasting. Burn all I have sketched!
The iron bar of conscience bends to gold;
Hard gold relaxes when seduced by heat;
Slight gunpowder can turn a king to dust,
And summer's breath fails with a little frost.
My whole life has been wasted.
(*Destroys sketchbook*)

All my paintings
Burn, that are not Christ's : for what is art,
And innate taste that cannot be acquired,
When man, the triumph of creation, turns
Into a jackal?

ALBIERA

Sandro, you are loved
By us caged birds who cannot fly so high.

SANDRO

See how the hawk towers the highest sky,
Views the vast earth, while somewhere, far below,
One speck, its trainer, waits; decides, in joy,
To leave limitless freedom and return
Down to the wrist from which it flew? A girl,
Grown into woman, of her own free will,
Visits her grandfather? So let me choose
To close my eyes, released from all life's chains,
And walk into the outstretched hands of God.

He dies.

EPILOGUE

ATROPOS, *alone.*

Horror intransigent,
Laughter and youth,
All that is transient
Teaches some truth.
Lost in life's meadow
Searching for love
Each one's a shadow
Thrown from above.
Find when, invisible,
I cut your fear,
Incomprehensible
Thought is made clear.
Atropos severs
Your threads, one by one :
All your endeavours
Are judged by the sun.
Here you have seen extremes;
All now's complete.
May you choose wisdom's dreams
Till next we meet.

FINIS

Renaissance Florence evoked in Radiant Poetry

Frank W. Dibb's review of Living Creation.

(THE STAGE, 9.v.85)

In *Living Creation*, jointly presented at its première in Oxford University's Examinations Schools by the University Experimental Theatre Club and the Oxford High School for Girls, Francis Warner, the Oxford poet and dramatist, has given vivid expression to the civic and religious conflicts of the Medicis, Savonarola, and their contemporaries in renaissance Florence.

Much of the action concerns Botticelli's creation of some of his masterpieces—shown in coloured-slide projections—their impact on his fellow Florentines and Savonarola's impassioned, vitriolic invective spoken in embittered, puritanical vein—almost reminiscent of John Knox at his most fulminatory.

Mr. Warner, in language that is invariably compulsive and heightened by the richness of sensitive, forceful imagery, has brought to the stage the intrigue, the religious sourness, the savage cruelty and also the beauty of the Florence of the Medicis.

Botticelli, as will be gathered, is a key character, seen constantly striving for the re-creation of beauty, and he was acted with a convincing degree of warmth by Martin Whitworth.

Inescapably riveting was the Lorenzo de Medici of Mark Payton, a recent recruit to the professional theatre from the ranks of the OUDS.

Payton has a magnetic stage presence, speaks with unfailing musicality—with a keenly developed feeling for the verse. He moves with care and precision. Here is a young, developing talent well worth considering as a future Hamlet.

Robert Wynford Evans gave lacerating expression to Savonarola's tirades against corruption. The producer was Greta Verdin.